P OE

of Yesteryear

Part II

Chips Barber

Sally Barber

Best wishes!
Chips Barber.

OBELISK PUBLICATIONS

Also by the Author

The Lost City of Exeter / The Great Little Exeter Book
The Ghosts of Exeter / Beautiful Exeter
Topsham Past and Present
Around & About the Haldon Hills–Revisited
Diary of a Dartmoor Walker / Diary of a Devonshire Walker
The Great Little Dartmoor Book / The Great Little Totnes Book
Made in Devon / Burgh Island and Bigbury Bay
Dark & Dastardly Dartmoor / Weird and Wonderful Dartmoor
Tales of the Teign / The Great Little Chagford Book
Ten Family Walks on Dartmoor / Ten Family Walks in East Devon
Six Short Pub Walks on Dartmoor
The Great Little Plymouth Book / Plymouth in Colour
Ghastly and Ghostly Devon / Dawlish and Dawlish Warren
The South Hams / Beautiful Dartmoor
Torquay / Paignton / Brixham
Around & About Salcombe / Around & About Seaton and Beer
Around & About Sidmouth / Around & About Teignmouth and Shaldon
From the Dart to the Start / Dartmouth and Kingswear
Cranmere Pool – the First Dartmoor Letterbox
Haunted Pubs in Devon
Brixham of Yesteryear Parts I, II and III
Teign Valley of Yesteryear Parts I and II
Princetown of Yesteryear Parts I and II

We have over 130 Devon titles; for further details please send a 1st class stamp to Obelisk Publications at the address below, or telephone (01392) 468556

This book is dedicated to the memory of Alan Somerwill

Acknowledgments

Many thanks to everyone who has kindly let me see and use their pictures of Pinhoe, including Joe Rogers, Joan Rogers, Cyril Vinnicombe, Mr Potter, Ron Brealy, Ann Webber, Ken and Jean Maun, Avril Spiller, Mrs Evelyn Lamacraft, Pat Peek, Mr Sid Stamp, D. Clarke, Mr and Mrs David Pickford, G. Knight, Arthur Hitchcock, Pat Salter, Mike Bennett, M. Martin, Mavis Piller, and Mr Harris. I would also like to thank everyone else who provided invaluable information but is not specifically mentioned here by name. Some of the more modern photos are reproduced by kind courtesy of Express and Echo Publications. Thanks to Rod Northcott for the cover picture.

First published in 1996 by
Obelisk Publications, 2 Church Hill, Pinhoe, Exeter, Devon
Designed by Chips and Sally Barber
Typeset by Sally Barber
Printed in Great Britain by
The Devonshire Press Limited, Torquay, Devon

PINHOE

of Yesteryear part 2

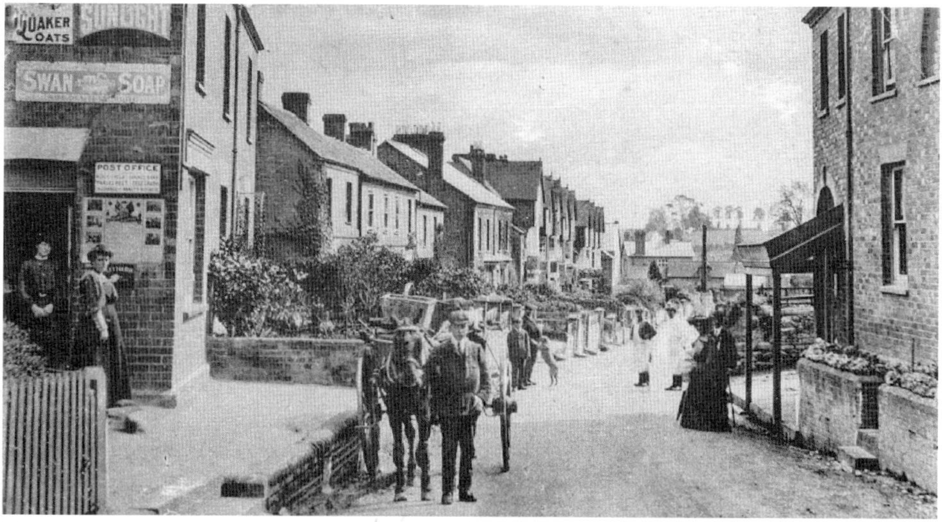

Here we go again for another trip down Pinhoe's very own 'Memory Lane'. I hope you will enjoy this further set of pictures that help to convey how things were in our village not that long ago.

An important building in Pinhoe is the post office in Station Road. The picture above shows part of it on the left hand side of the view with quite a few advertisement boards. There are no yellow lines for the horse and cart. Opposite, the building that houses the present-day launderette has a porch of sorts.

The second picture looks from the centre of the village towards the Heart of Oak.

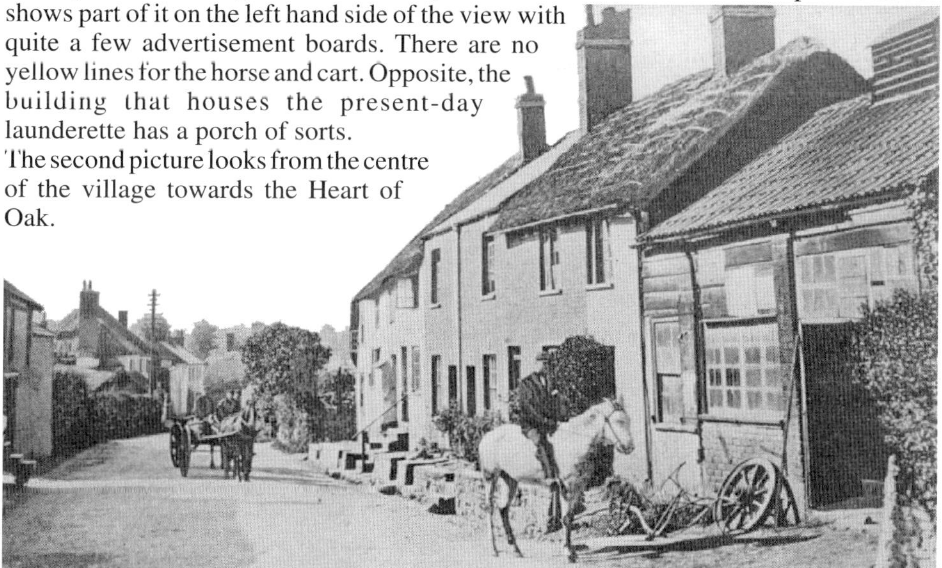

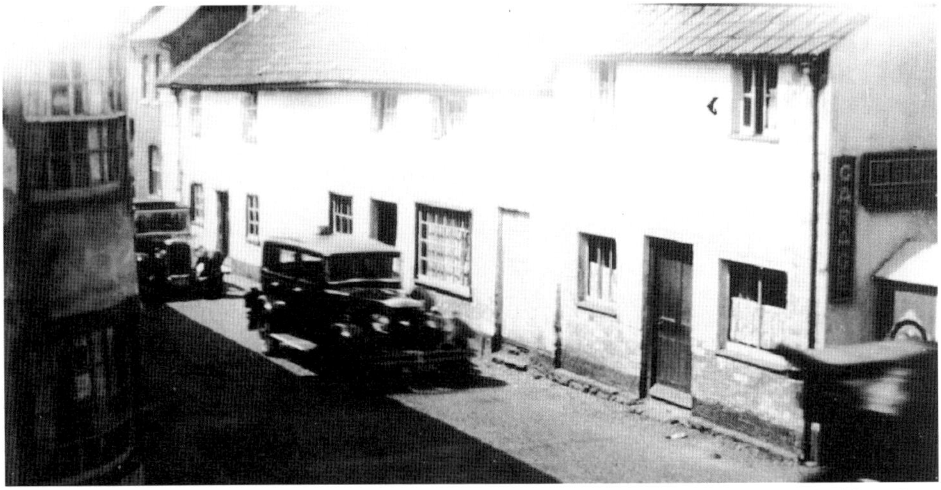

These two views were taken in opposite directions. The top picture was probably taken in a hurry when members of the Royal Family drove through the centre of Pinhoe on a bright sunny morning many years ago.

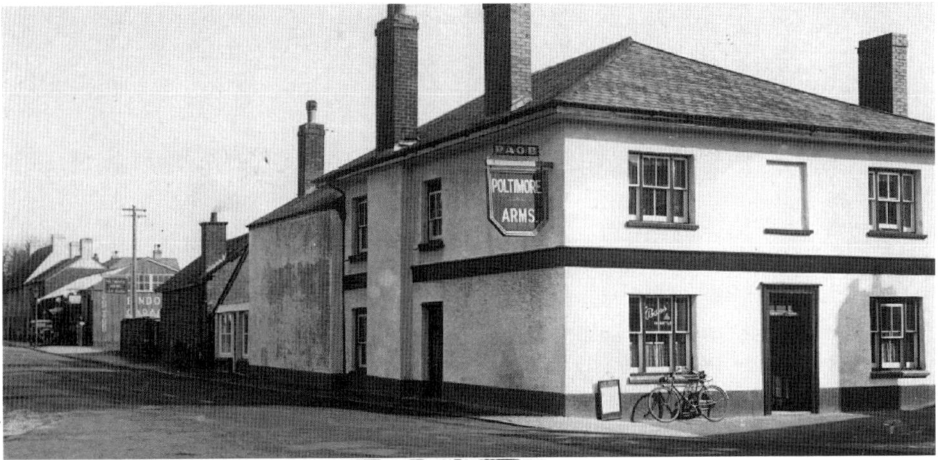

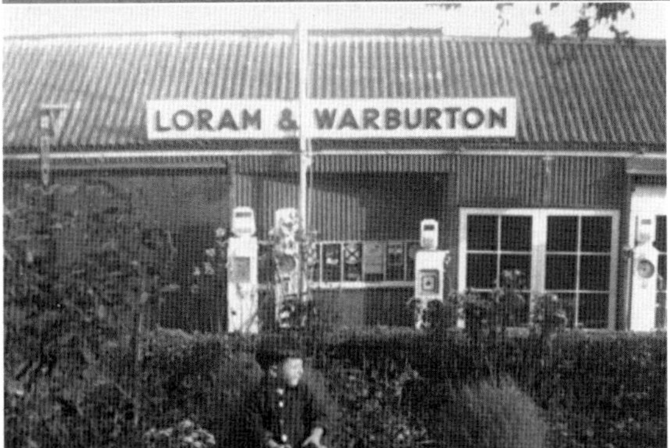

Above is the Poltimore Arms with no railings around the corner and an extra door on the Langaton Lane side of the building. It is likely that the owner of the bike, propped against the pub window, was refreshing himself. It's also likely that he didn't need to padlock it either!

(Left) This picture shows the original version of the other garage further along Main Road, towards Broadclyst.

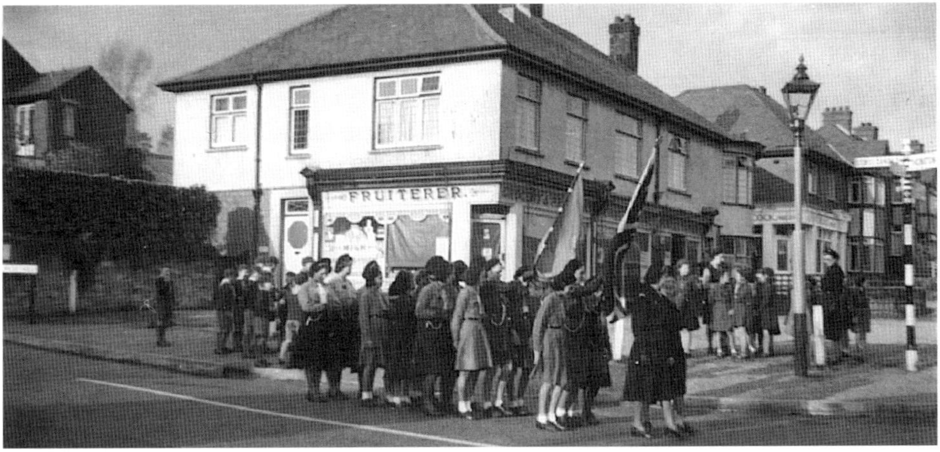

The parade has just come down Church Hill to reach the centre of Pinhoe. Behind them the corner of the main road looks very different without Joe Rogers' ironmonger's shop. Below is the centre of Pinhoe in those days of transition when the horse hadn't quite given away to the automobile. The angles of the vehicles and the assembled crowd might suggest some sort of traffic incident – it certainly looks slippery! If you look closely you will observe that the Poltimore Arms has its pub sign at the top of a tall pole.

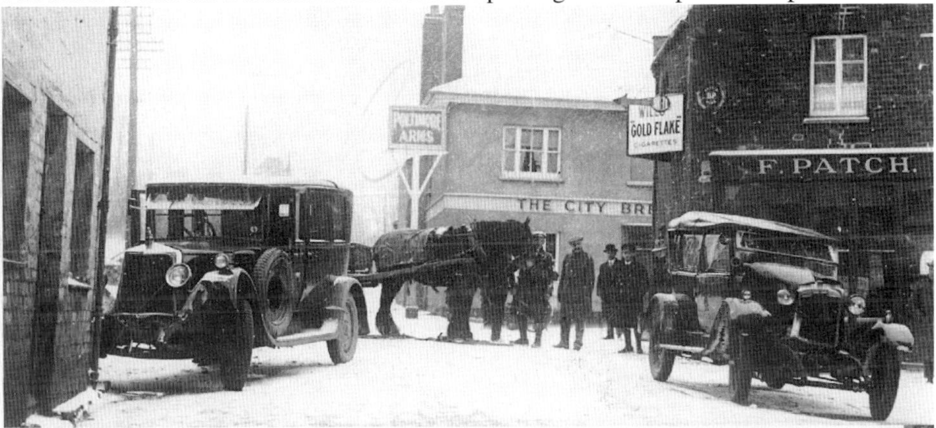

Pinhoe's other pub, the Heart of Oak, is featured below with no bus shelters to break a clean run of buildings. There is no traffic, save a static car parked on the pavement by the inn.

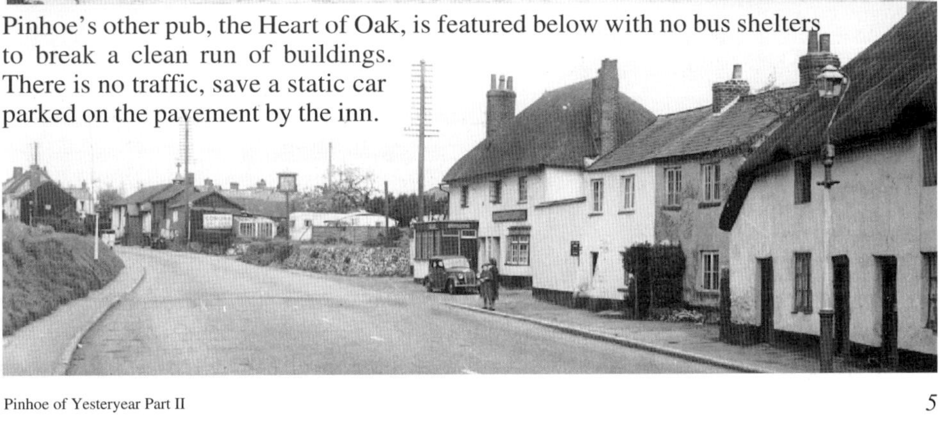

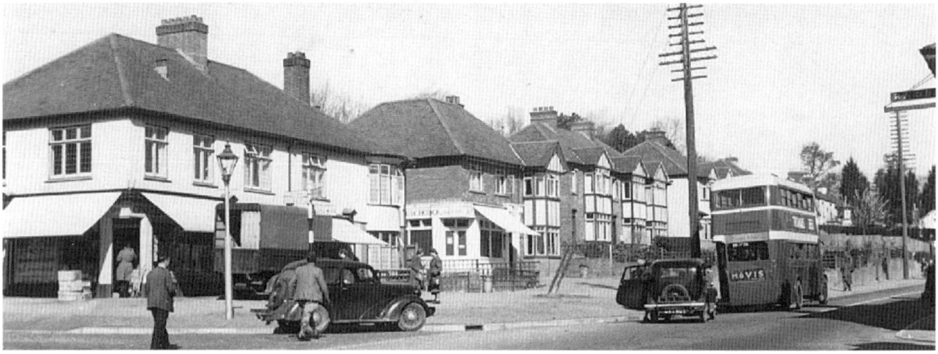

Although there is traffic in the above picture it looks less cluttered than it does today with no railings, no mini roundabouts, a smaller supermarket. The bottom picture is the opposite view to the one above but taken many years earlier when the Pinhoe Garage stood on this important junction and where Mr Patch's motor mechanics could 'patch up' your automobile. The Main Road was much narrower and if you look at this and the two on the opposite page you will see that Patrolman Cotton managed to get into many pictures. His 'box' can be seen in the centre of the bottom picture.

After the first *Pinhoe of Yesteryear* several people recalled fond memories of the cottages shown just left of the centre of this (middle) picture. The same spot is now where the present Pinhoe Garage displays its cars for sale. Years ago a number of residents from the south side of Main Road would carry their washing over the road and hang it on washing lines in the front gardens of these houses. It appears that this arrangement evolved because their own gardens were too small and too shady.

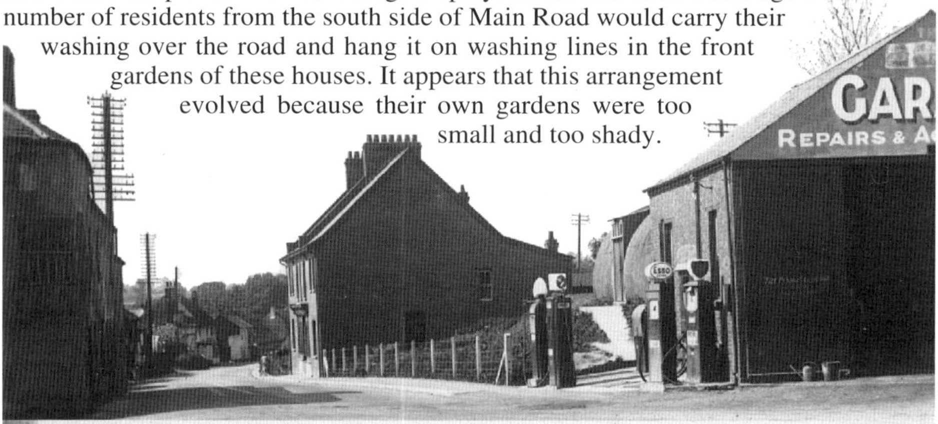

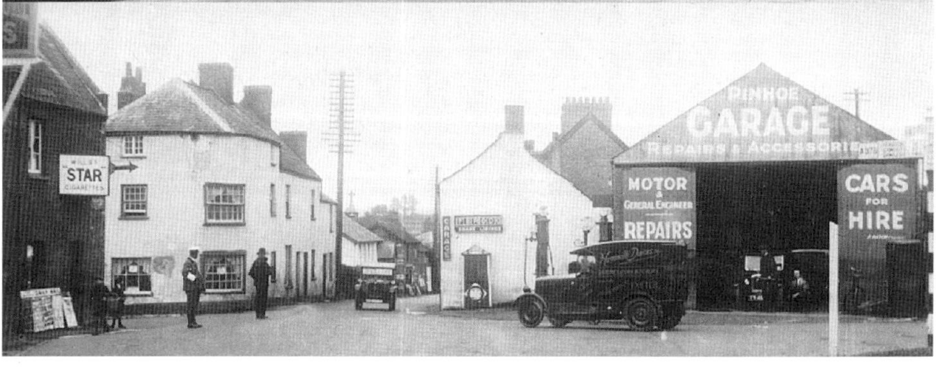

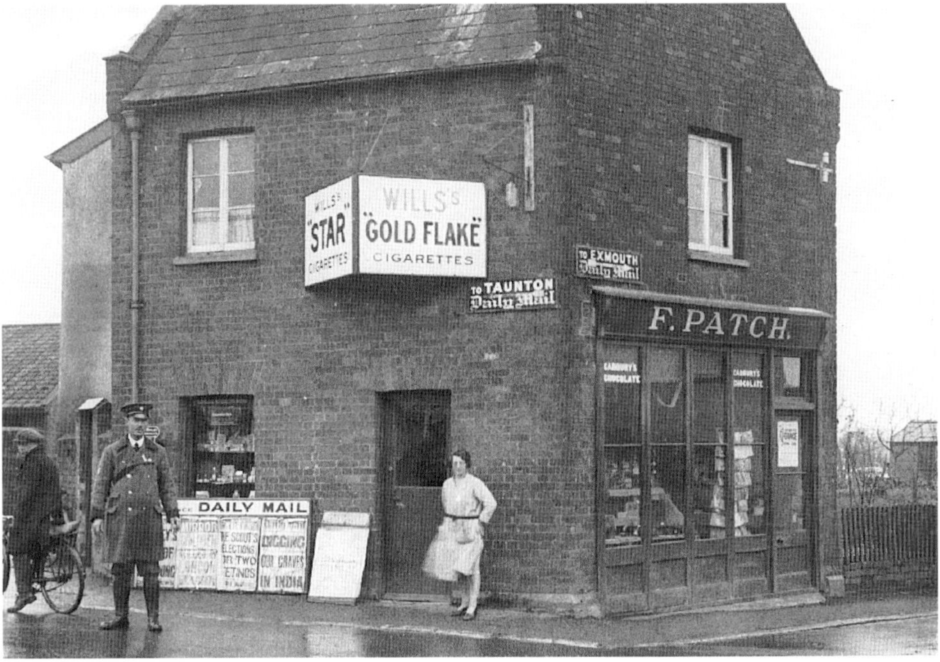

Mrs Tabitha Patch is seen here, standing outside Patch's shop, which stood between Langaton Lane and Station Road, almost on the site of Pearson's Supermarket. Note the direction boards on the side of the building. By courtesy of the *Daily Mail* motorists could glance up and see the way to Taunton or to Exmouth.

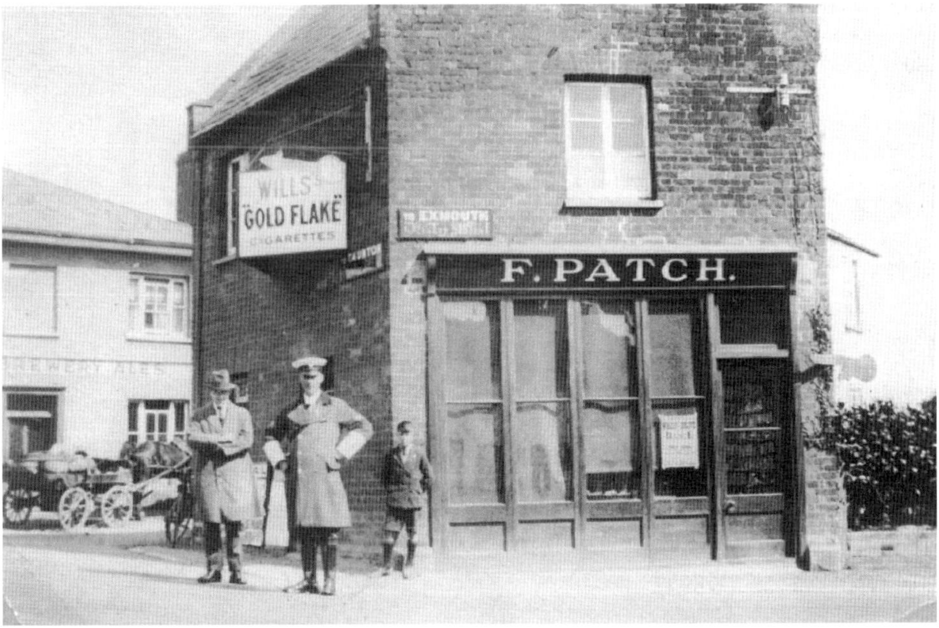

Mrs Patch is seen here passing a tray over the fence in her back garden at a VE Day party. If you look carefully, the bottom house in Church Hill is just visible in the top left corner.

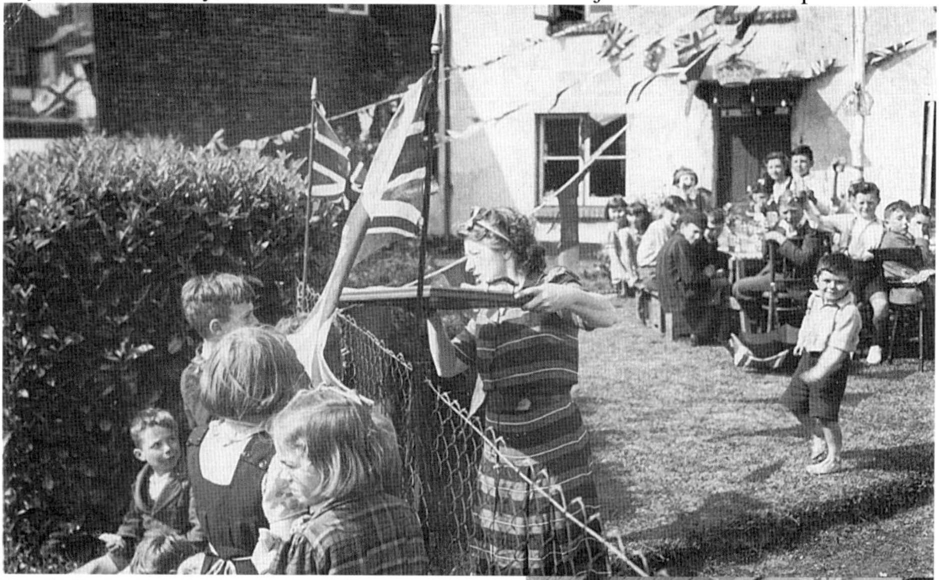

Frank Rogers took over the original newsagency business after the retirement of his mother, Daisy Rogers. The shop was rebuilt in 1961 and by the time of his death in 1982 he had bought the Hardware Stores and the Station Road newsagency. Two windows in Pinhoe church were commissioned in his memory by his wife Rosemarie.

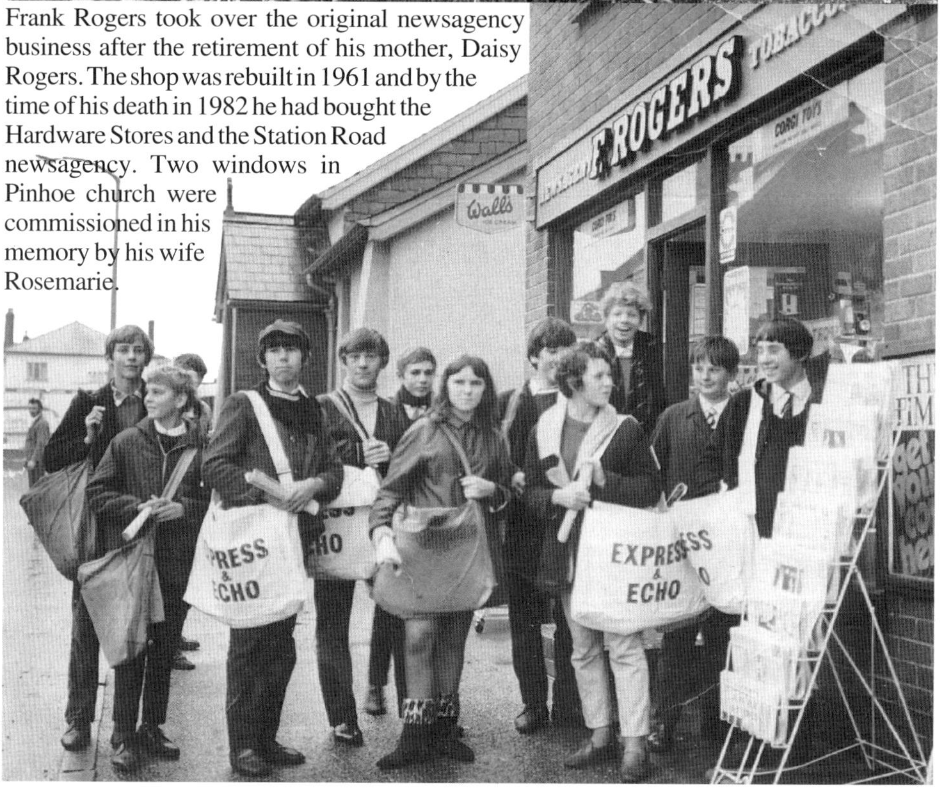

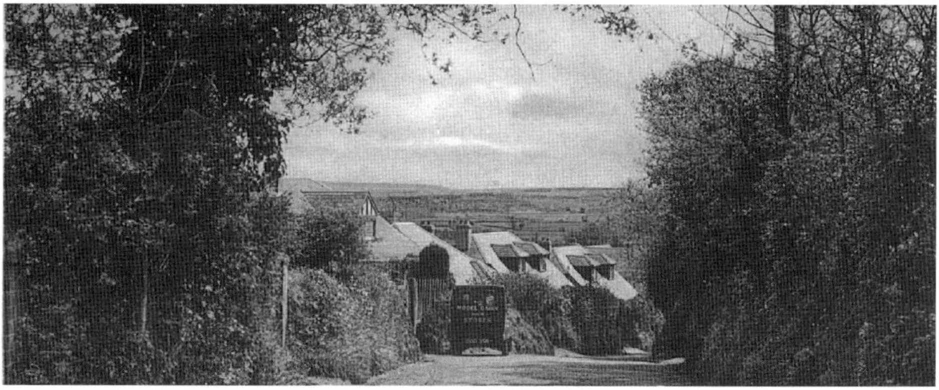

The top picture is looking down Park Lane and the single vehicle belonged to Freddie Pyle who ran the Model Dairy, from what is now the site of the Spar shop.

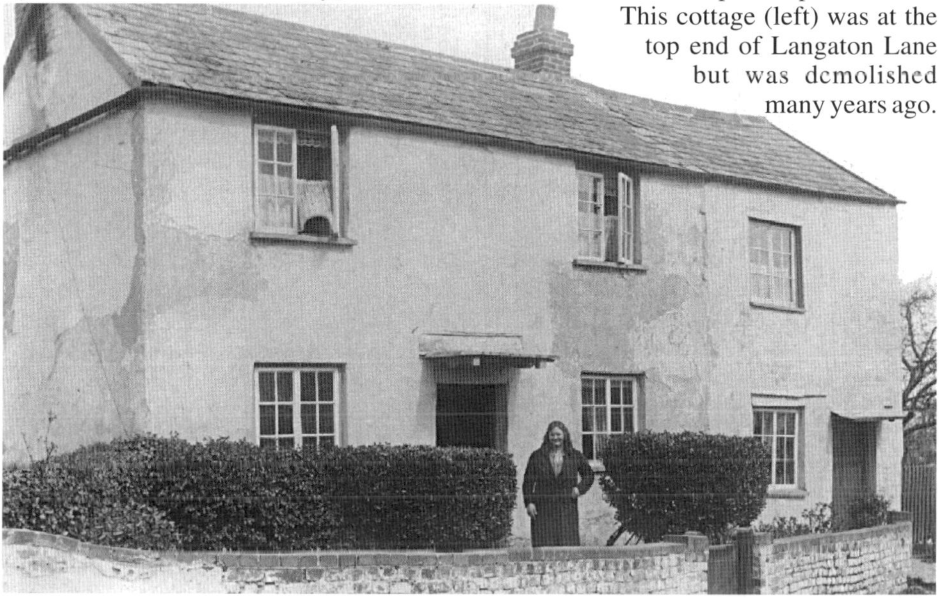

This cottage (left) was at the top end of Langaton Lane but was demolished many years ago.

The view below is looking up Langaton Lane. The cottages on the right became one big building when a lady moved there from Hatherleigh so named her new home Hatherleigh!

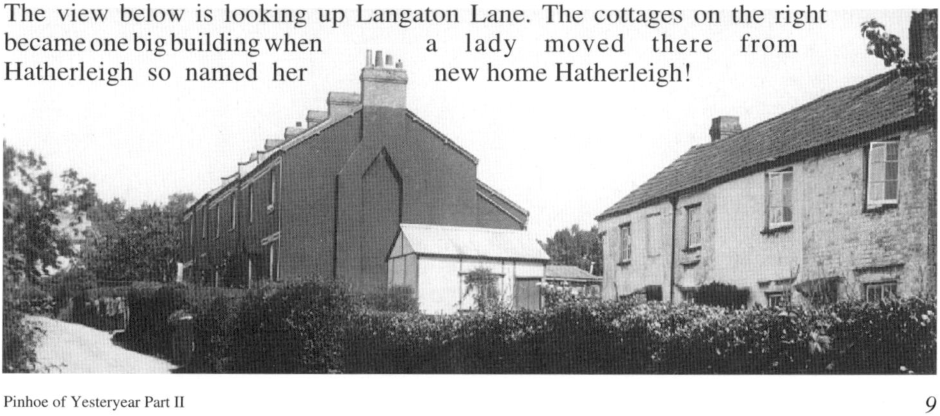

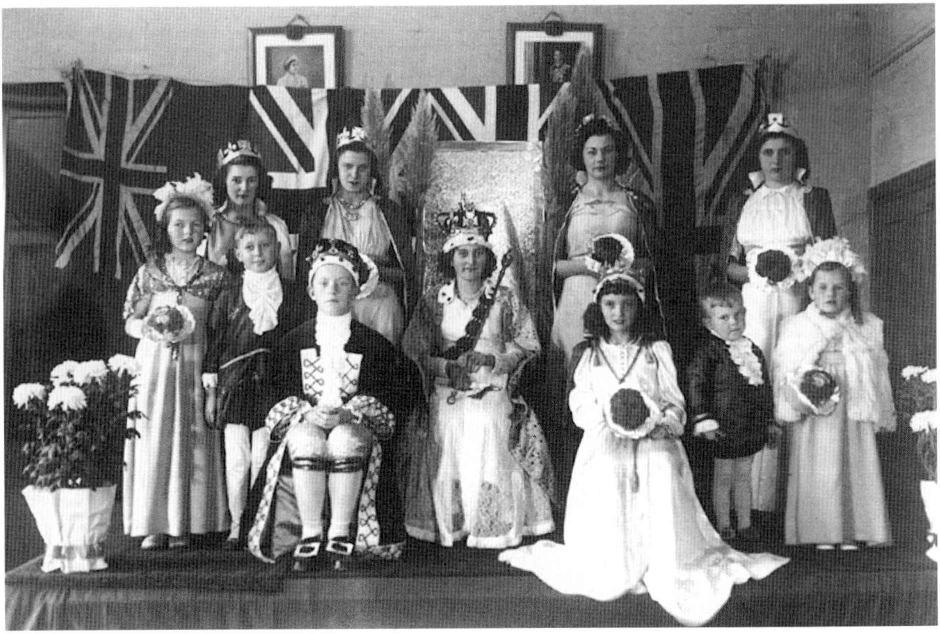

Here we have a touch of royalty in Pinhoe. The Pinhoe Carnival Queen is Helen Bauer, her noble prince is a young Arthur Hitchcock. Taken in September 1947, the picture also includes John Lugg, the Kerswell twins, Brian and Beryl, Pam Holding, Pat Taylor, 'Princess' Yvonne Rogers, Beattie Pearce and Margaret Snow.

When such a large crowd appear in so small a picture as the one below it's hard to pick out individuals posing in front of the Big Top. This was taken in the same field where the fair has been held in recent years, just beyond Venny Bridge.

Unfortunately the photographer didn't manage to get all of everyone into the top picture opposite and the original was not in focus. However, it shows the ladies of the WI's drama group and include the following ladies in the back row: Mesdames Causley, Orton, Warren, Gumm, Cazer and Salter. The front row includes Mrs Tripe, Marion Cowling and Mrs Smith.

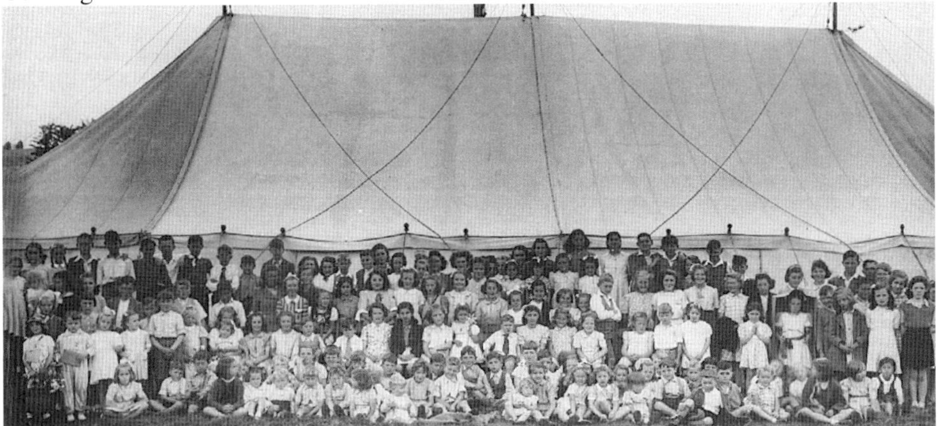

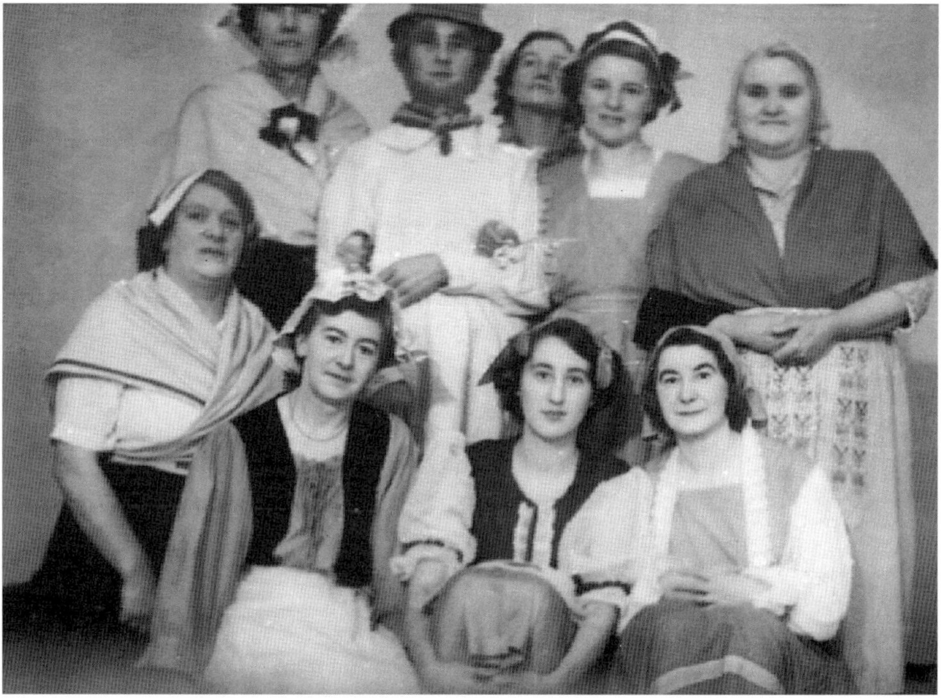

Below is Pinhoe's Home Guard as they looked in 1940. Although the list is not complete, included in the photo are the following personnel – Front row: Bob Siddons, Les Steer, Sgt Marles, Living, Harold Salter, Major Jackson, Holliwell, C. Causley, Bob Melhuish, Brealey, C. Cazer. Middle row: A. Hodgers, Harold Garnsworthy, Stan Wigg, A. Scoble, Cyril Snow, Webber, Les M, Wilf Browning, Treas, Reg Cox. Back row: Peter Steer, Lionel May, Frank Chamberlain, Bill Rowsel, 'Rev Ley', Sid Loss, Horace Barker, Percy Butt, Doug Howe.

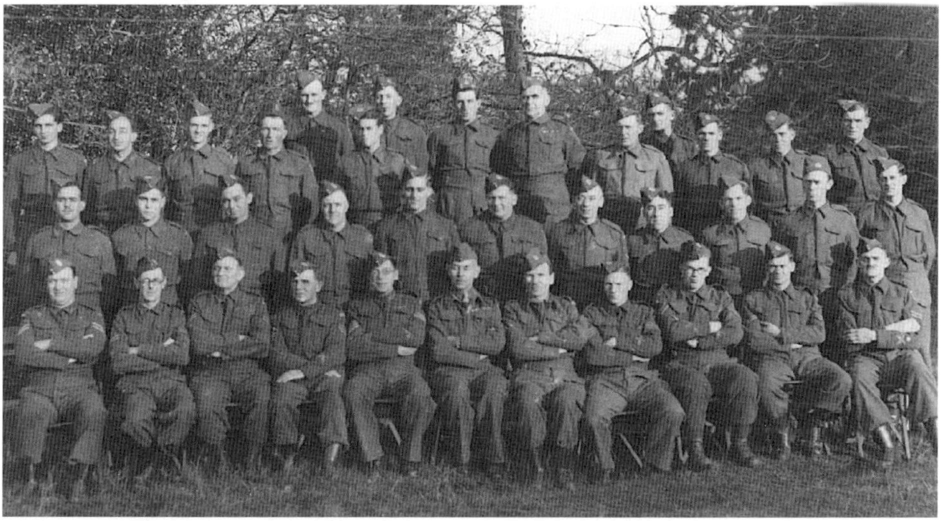

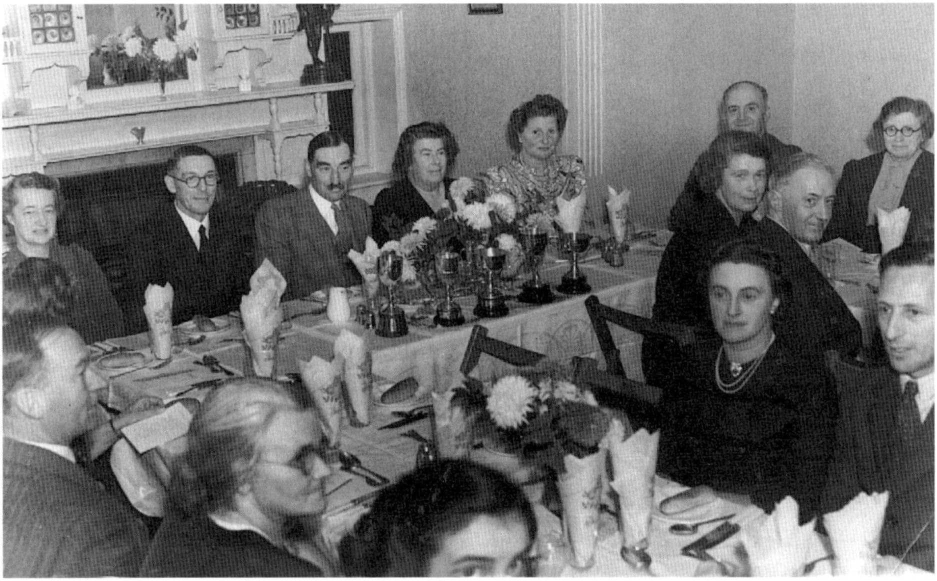

This picture was taken at the large house known as Broadparks, now Overland Court, and divided into flats, at the top of Broadparks Avenue. This is a Rifle Club dinner – featured are Mr Harold Salter, his wife and daughter, Captain and Mrs Parker, and Dr Gipson. The picture below is also of the rifle club, showing them outside their former HQ at Monkerton. They are proudly showing off the Kynoch Shield, a prestigious trophy they won at Okehampton. The sewn on badges, on the jackets of the men standing, say Pinhoe.

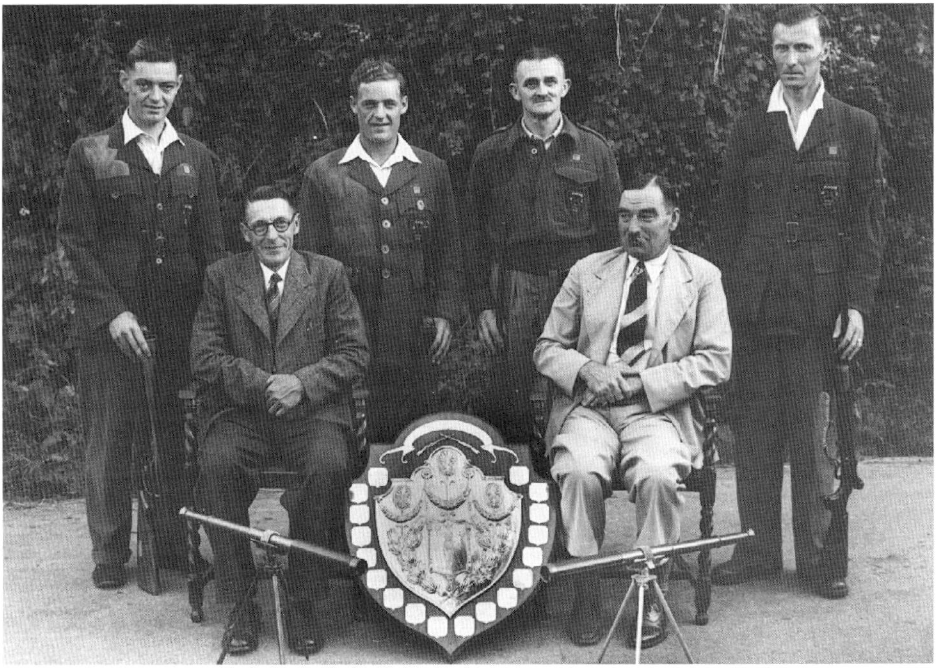

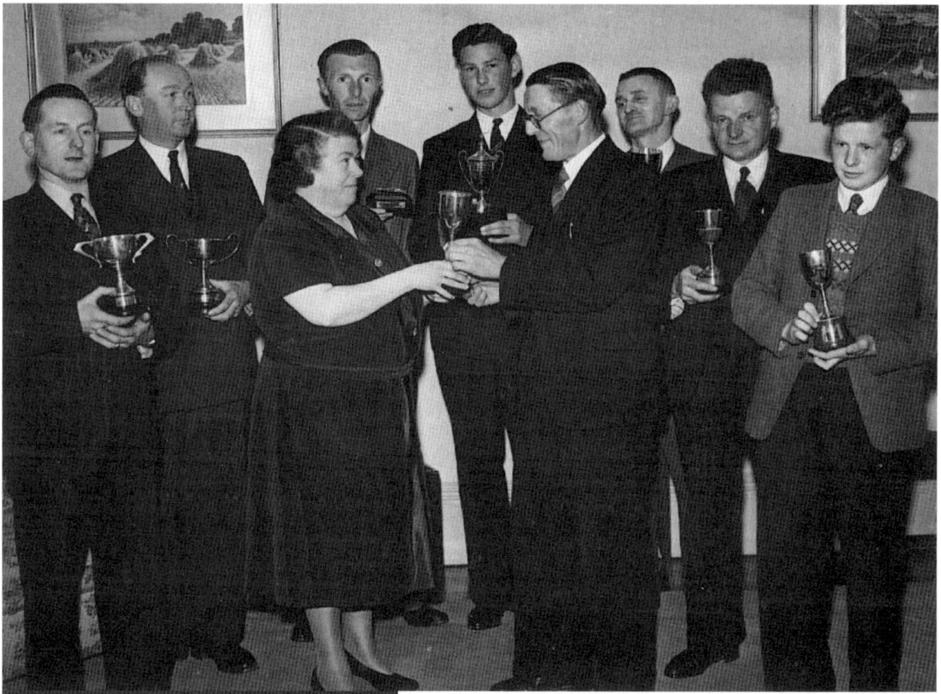

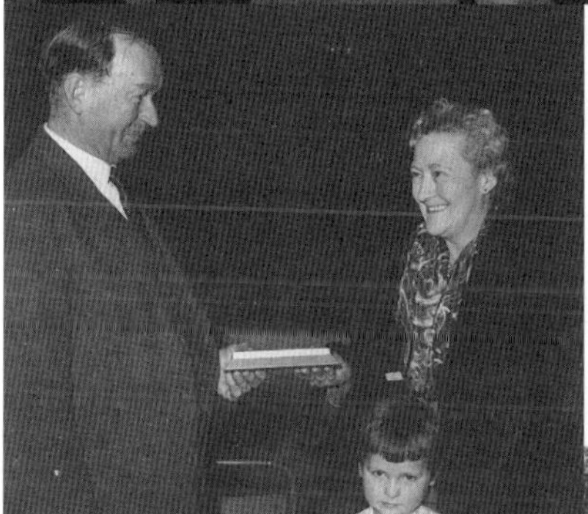

(Above) Mrs Parker is presenting an award to Harold Salter at the Rifle Club dinner at the Gipsy Hill Hotel. Also present in the photo are other trophy winners: Bob May, Dr Gipson, Dave Best, Stan Illsley, Cec Cazer, Reg Kerslake, Norman May. (Left) Taken in about 1962, this shows Dr Gipson making a farewell presentation to Nurse Early who emigrated to Australia. The little girl is Shirley Early. (Below) Harold Salter is tackling some maintenance work at the Rifle Club's original HQ.

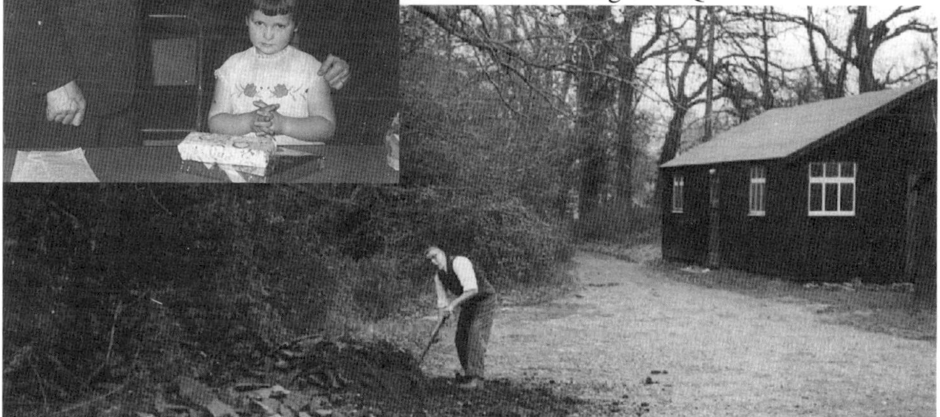

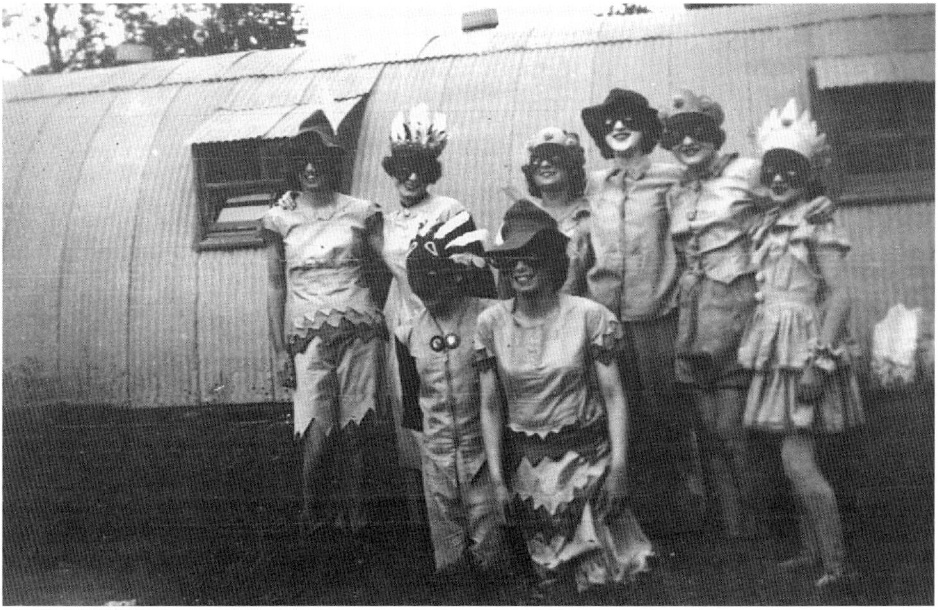

The Temporary Hut was just a stone's throw away and many imaginative productions were staged here and many dinner parties celebrated. Here we have Pinhoe's answer to the Lone Ranger, eight desperados incognito.

Below, camp has been struck and it's time for the youngsters to return from a life under canvas. The picture is taken in 1958 at the junction of Station Road and Causey Lane. This was before the houses were built.

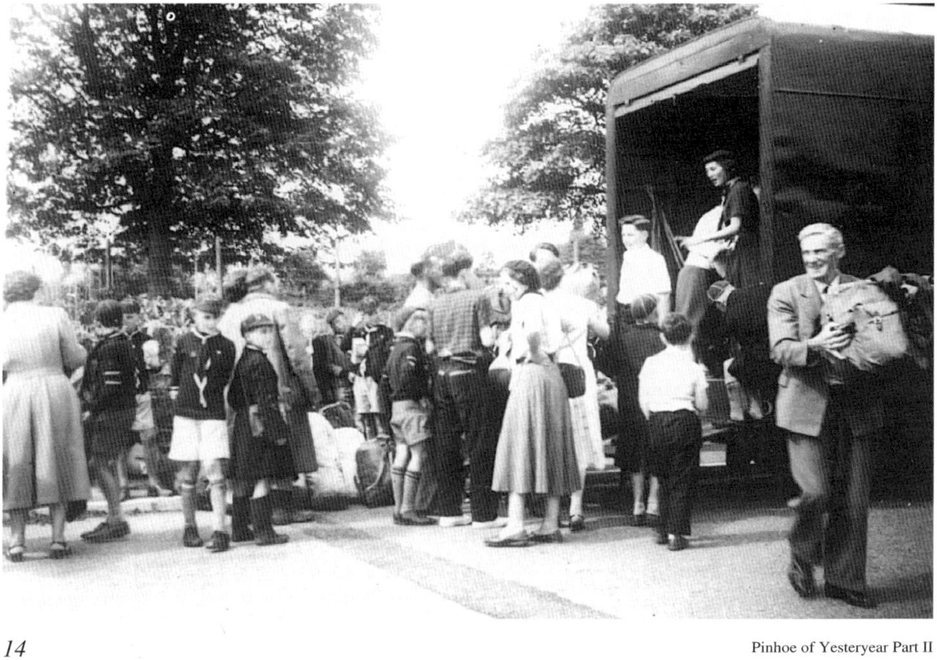

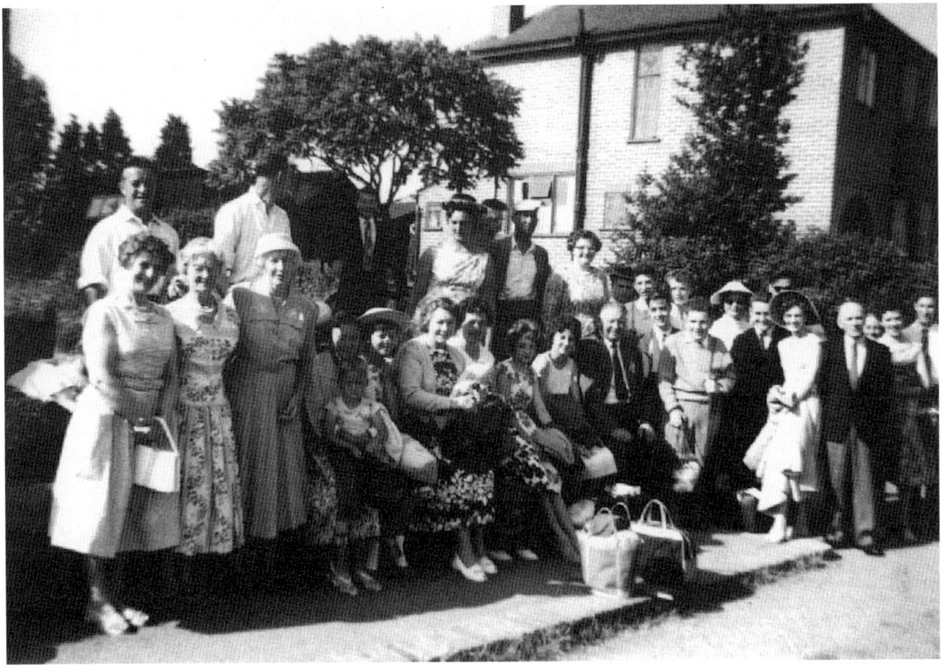

There's nothing more guaranteed to put a smile on people's faces than a good day out. The above picture is taken in Causey Lane and the one below at one of the destinations. Judging by the cheerful expressions and their summer attire, it looks like a good time was had by all on this summer outing.

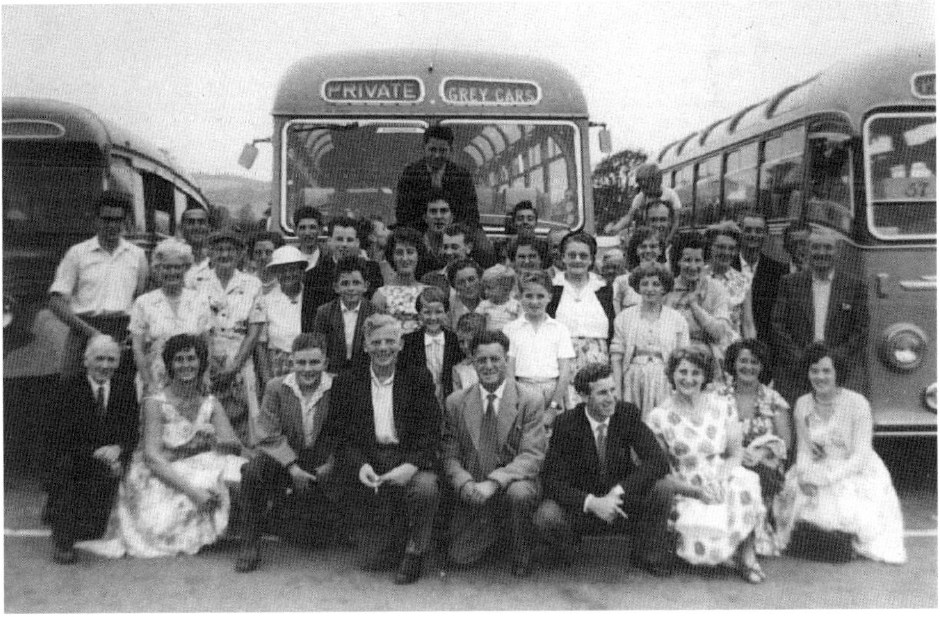

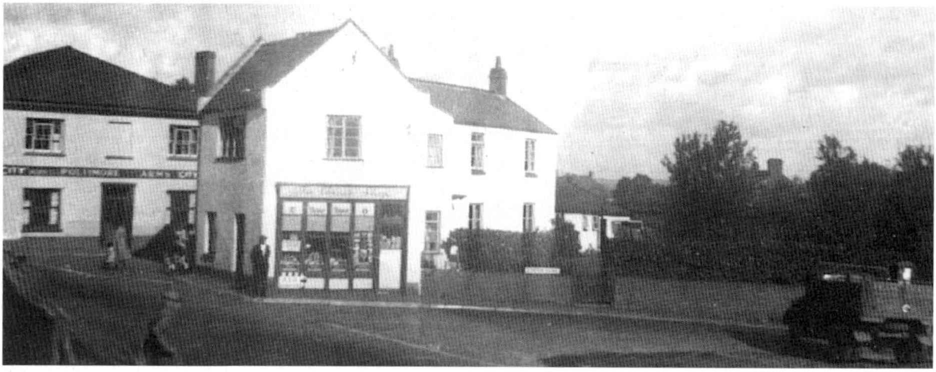

Above is another view of Patch's shop, on the corner of both Langaton Lane and Station Road. The middle view is looking across the forecourt in front of the present day Spar shop. The Poltimore Arms is on the left and Patch's garage is on the right.

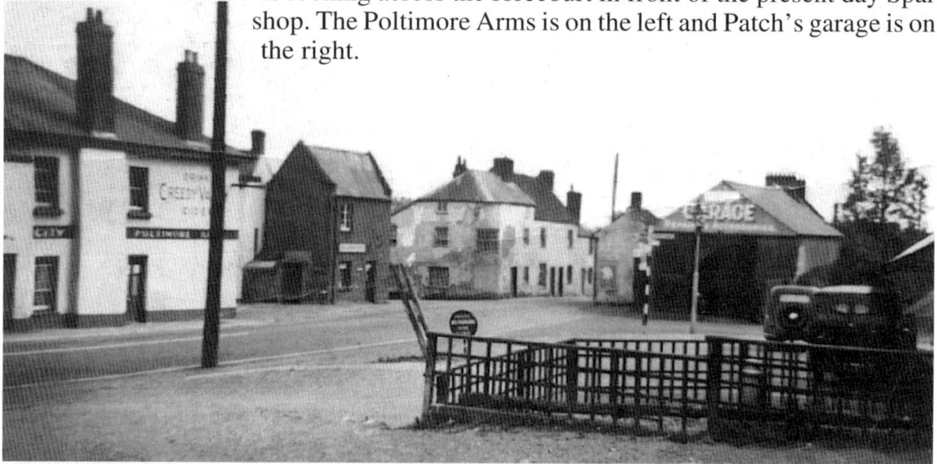

Here we see the demolition of cottages that were on the opposite top corner of station Road, now an open space. The intention was to build a supermarket here but this is one that was never built, despite initial planning permission.

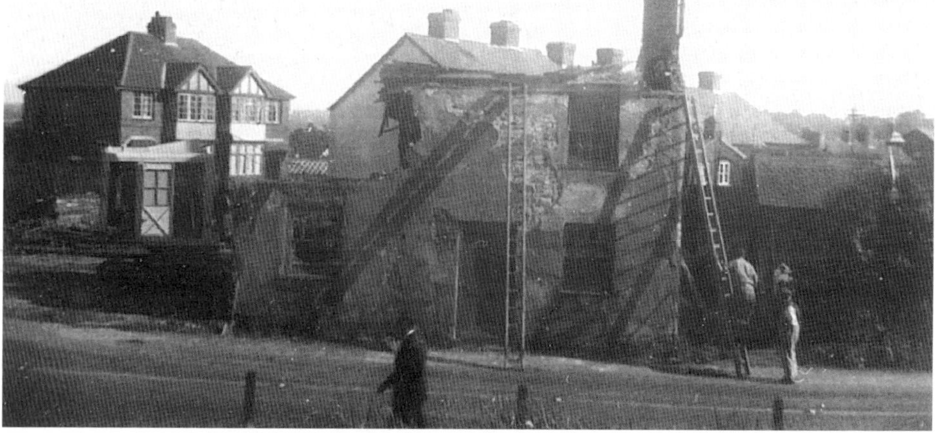

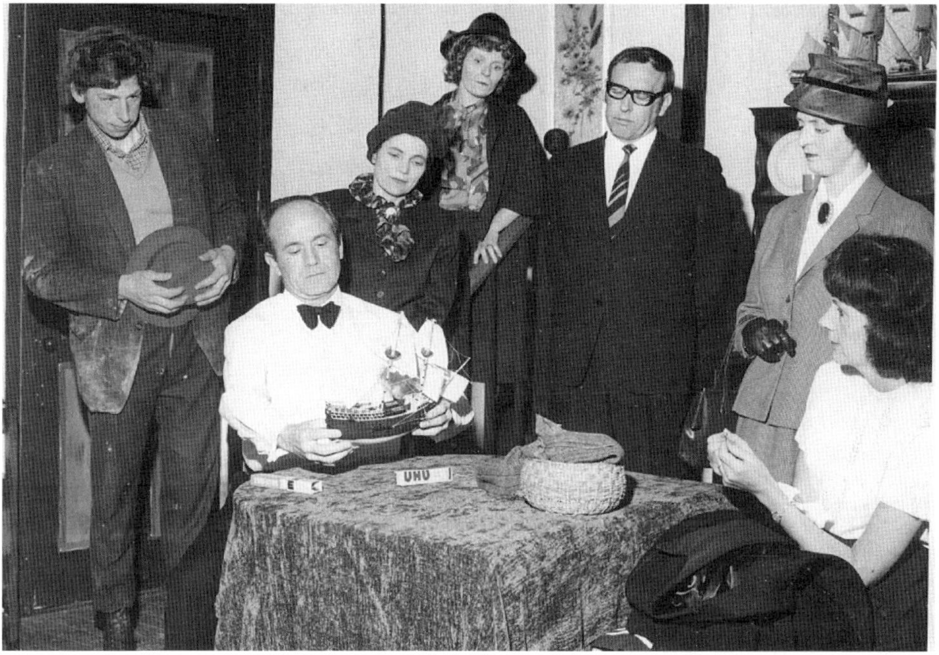

Above the Pinhoe Players act out a scene from 'The Secret Tent' which was performed in 1974. (L to R): Colin Patch, Colin Davey, Ann Webber, Jean Wilson, Gerry Norburn, Hannah Mortimore and Jill Chettle. Below we have moved on two years to the production of the ghost story 'The Paragon'. (L to R): Joyce Evans, Colin Davey, Ann Webber, Jean Wilson, John Fenwick, Gerry Norburn, Marion Cowling and Dick Foxen.

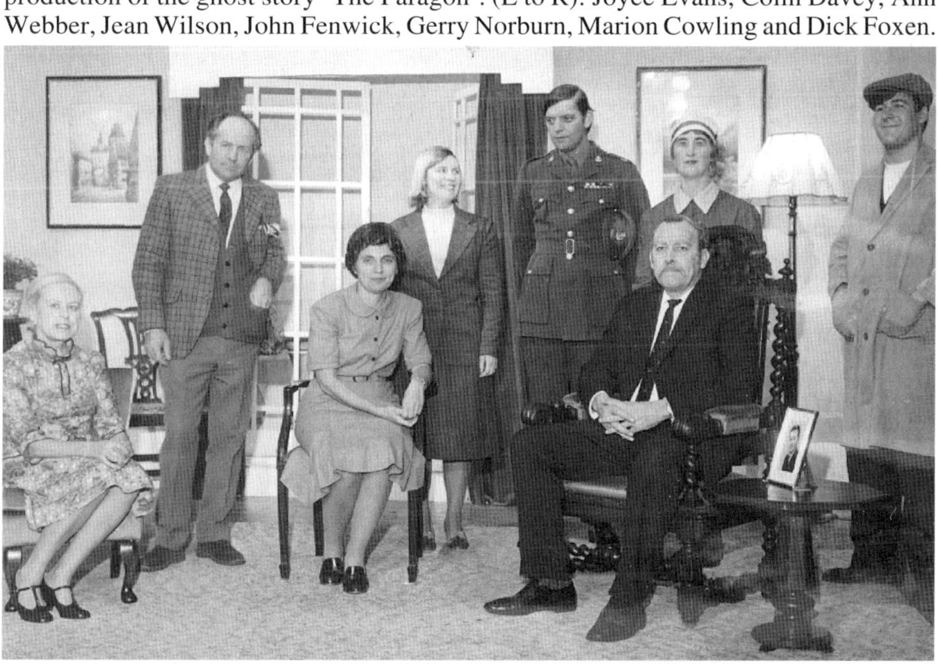

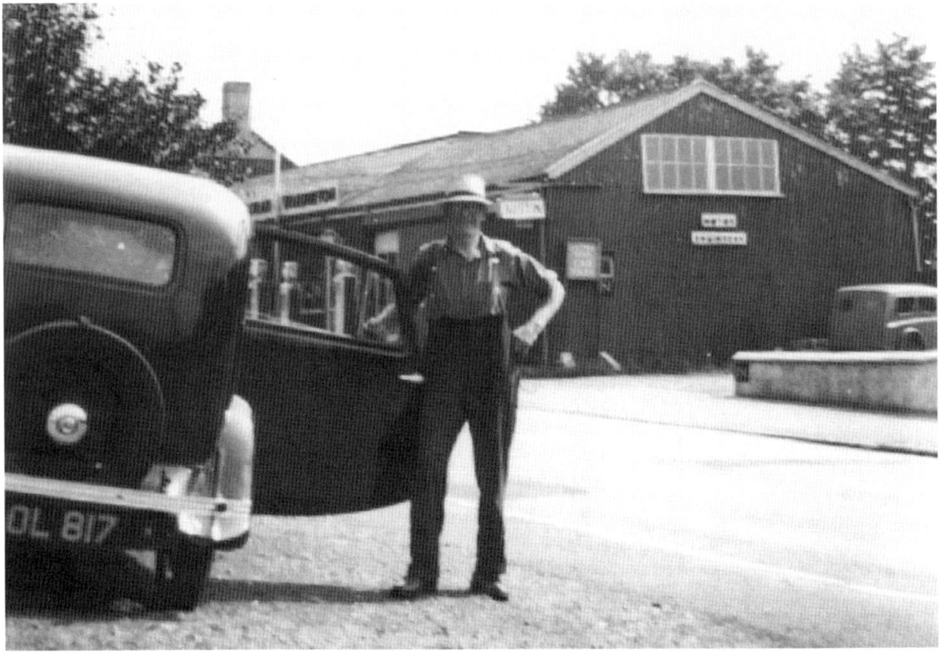

From the height of summer to the depths of winter. Here we have two similar views looking along the road towards what was Loram and Warburton's garage. The present day filling station's pumps are where the cottages are to be seen in the lower picture. The Hitchcock twins can be seen, with their father, Arthur, enjoying the snowy scene outside their dad's butcher shop. The picture was taken in 1963 by Mr Coates.

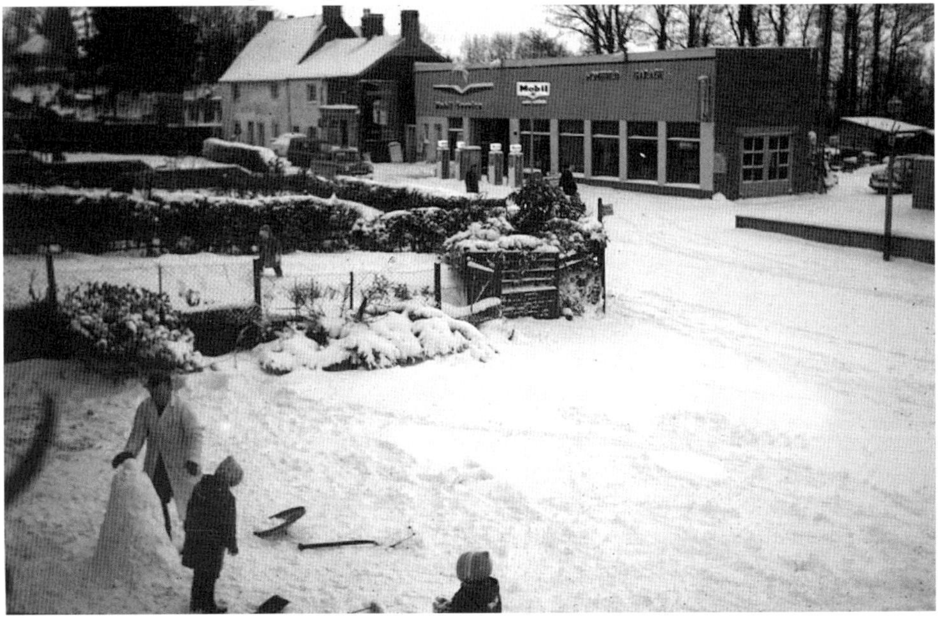

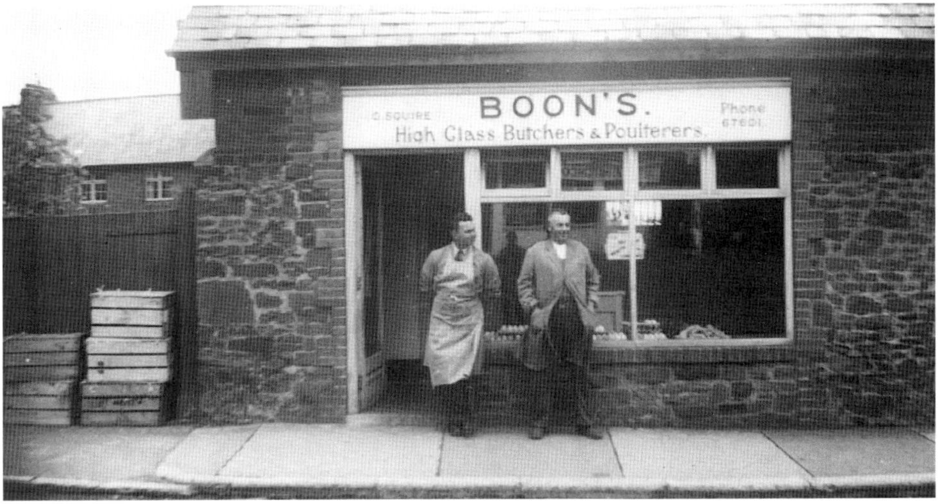

Above is a picture of the building that now houses Po Lee's Chinese takeaway. As will be seen from this picture, the building was originally single storey.

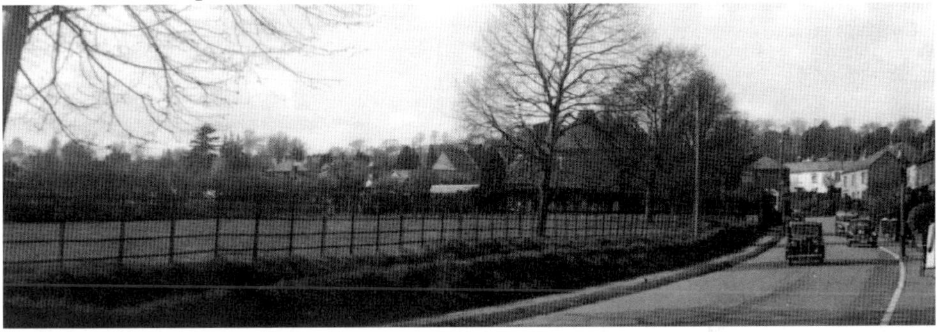

This picture shows the extent of the green field in Station Road which, until the building of houses, would have made a pleasant outlook for those who lived along here.

Below is an outing to Cheddar Gorge in an open-top charabanc. In those days it was a long journey but the traffic was far less, so it was probably a pleasant day out for those involved.

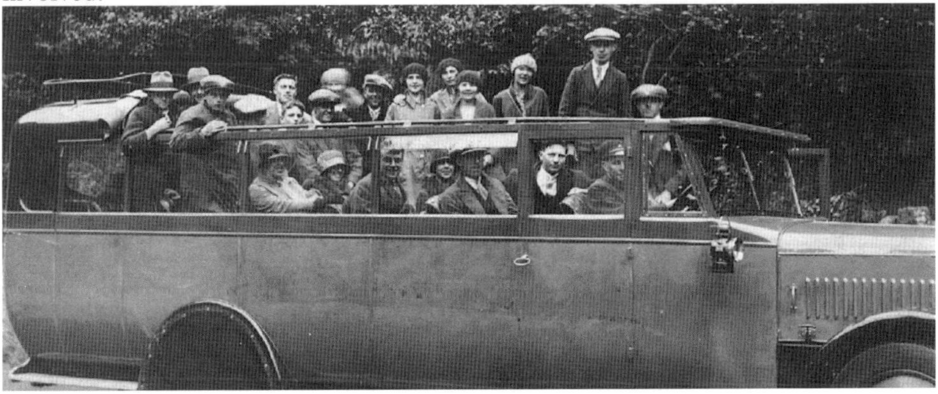

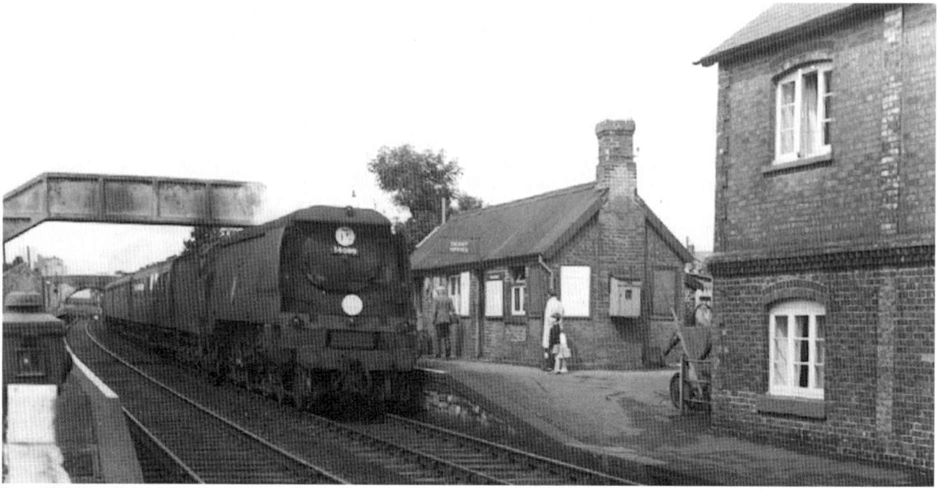

In the first volume of *Pinhoe of Yesteryear* we featured a couple of pictures of Pinhoe's railway station, one an earlier view and another from its reopening in 1983. These two views, taken by rail enthusiast, Ronald A. Lumber, date from between those two pictures. The one above dates back to 18 August 1964 and shows more station buildings than exist today. Note the footbridge, partly obscured by locomotive number 34080's steam, that linked the two platforms. The view below looks the other way towards the level crossing. It was taken 22 May 1965 and shows the last steam train, working out of Exmouth Junction, to stop at Pinhoe having travelled from Axminster. The station closed to passenger traffic in early March 1966.

The first signal box, originally with only one storey, was the detached house, which stands by the crossing, where a suitable theme tune might well have been "The railroad runs through the middle of the house". As the station grew it was vertically enlarged to become the stationmaster's home and another signal box was built opposite.

Modern technology means that there is no longer a signal box at Pinhoe. The signal box

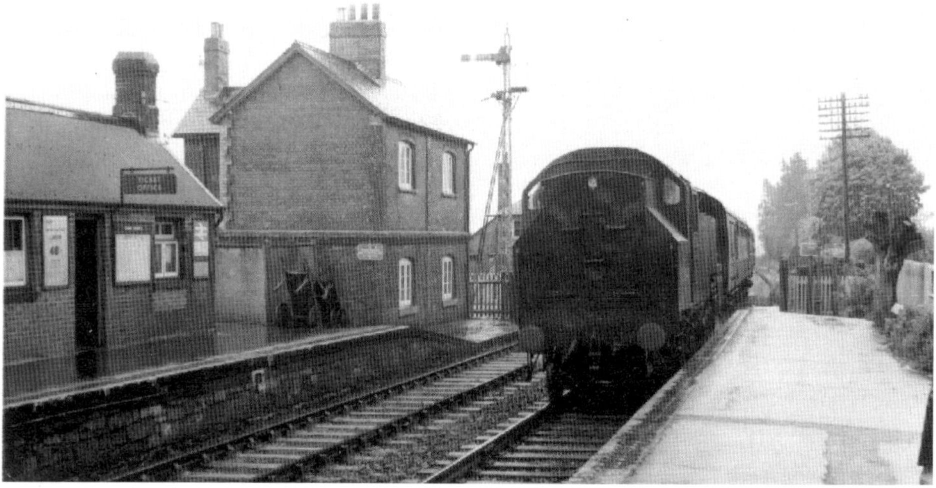

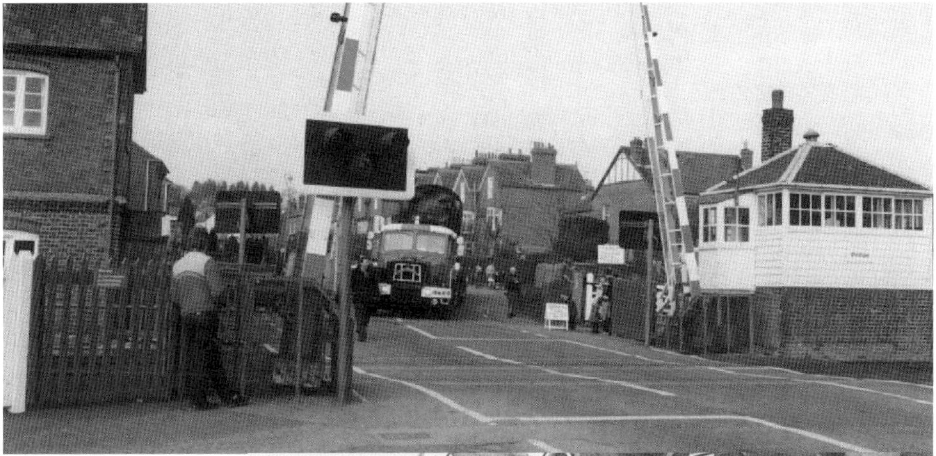

was uprooted and transported to Bere Ferrers, a station on the beautiful branch line from Plymouth, up the Tamar valley to Gunnislake and, although it appears to be part of the railway's furniture is, in fact, in the grounds of the station now converted to a private dwelling. The picture below shows where it now stands.

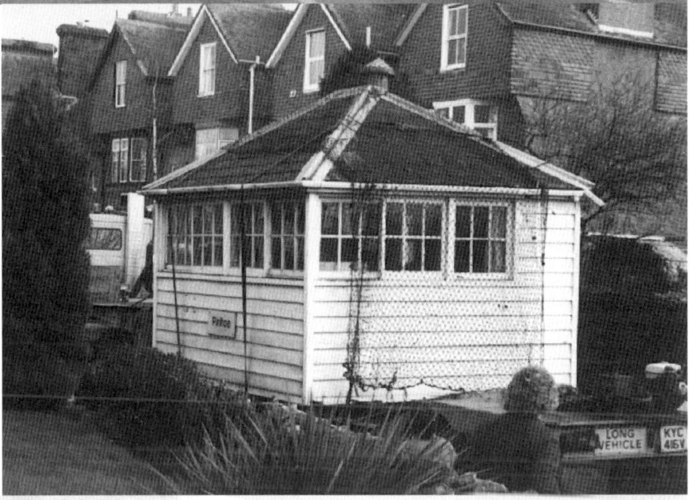

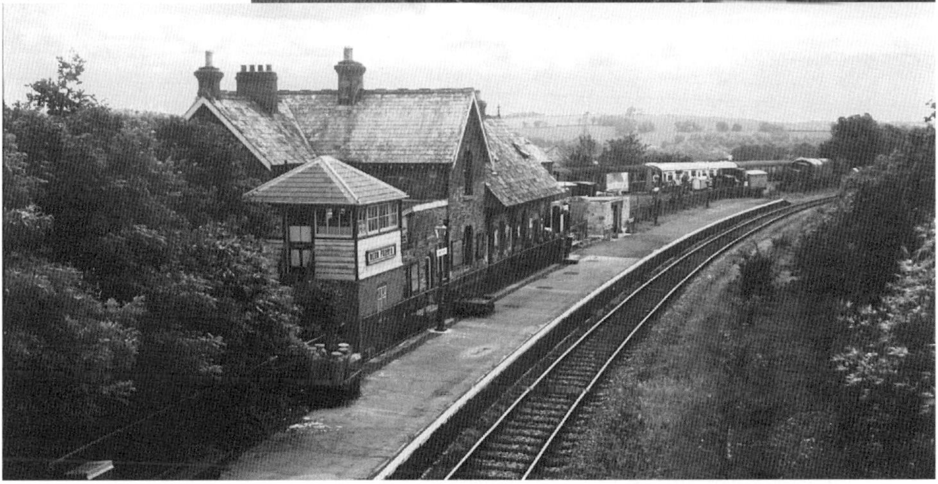

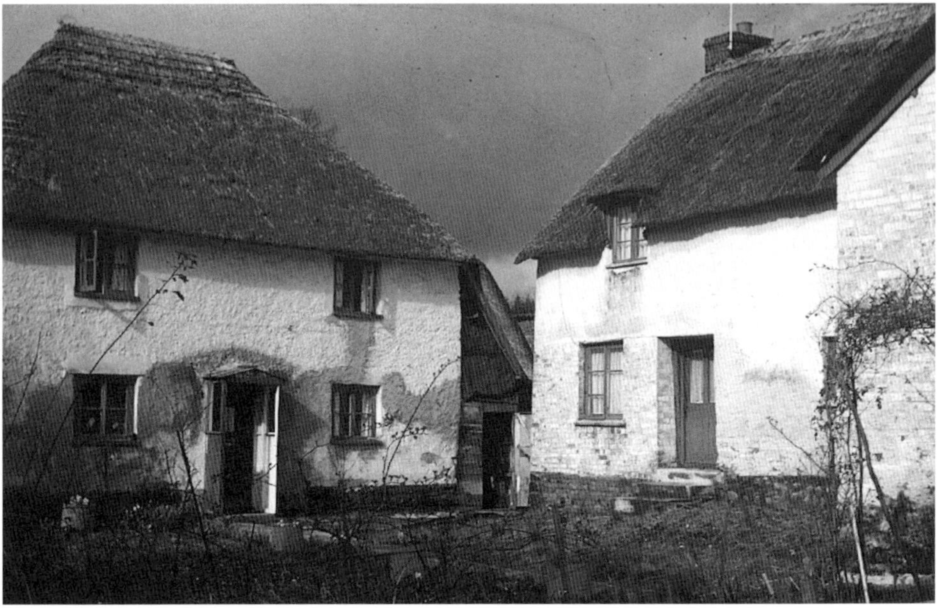

Some scenes change greatly whilst others just adapt to modern needs. Above are attractive cottages which stood beside Harrington Lane, more or less where Harrington Gardens is today. Their fate was sealed when they burnt down which helped solve a dilemma as they needed a lot of work done to them. The terrace below is clearly recognisable as Causey Lane, taken before the age of replacement windows!
The top picture opposite is of a fire at Banks Place, a name that will mean nothing to most folks. This is the part of Pinhoe Road which branches off left into Venny Bridge. As will be seen from the photo, the fire razed most of its buildings to the ground.

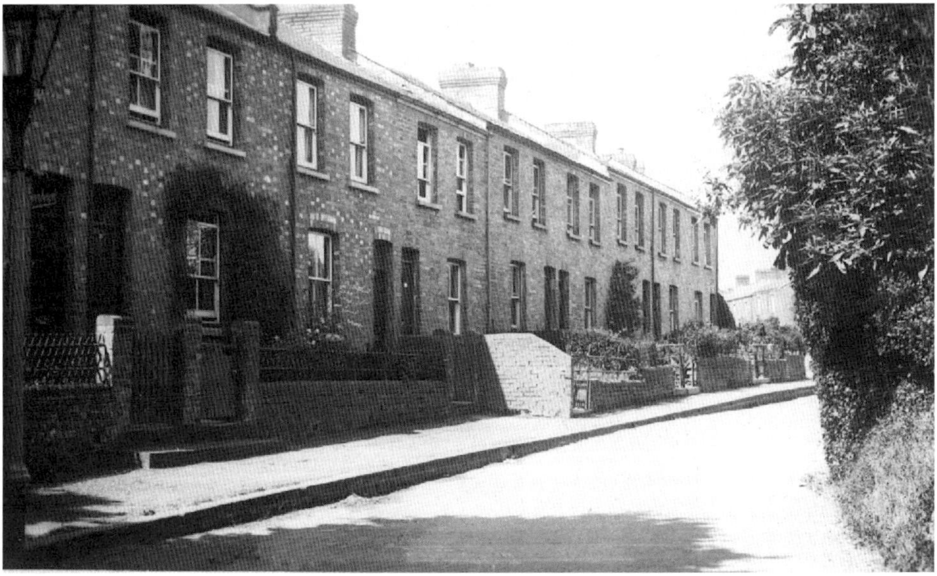

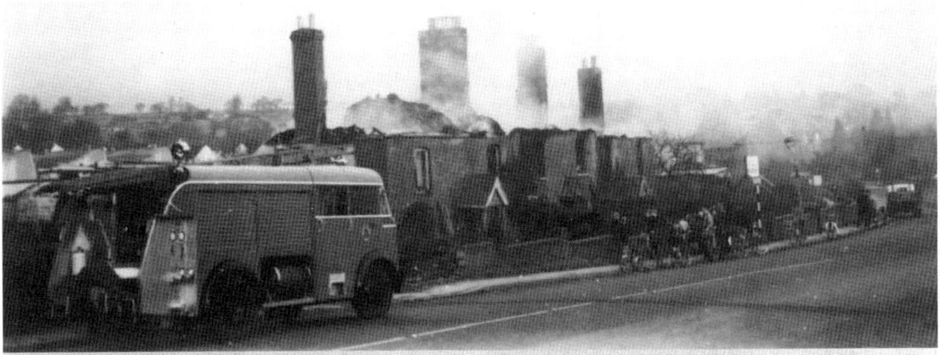

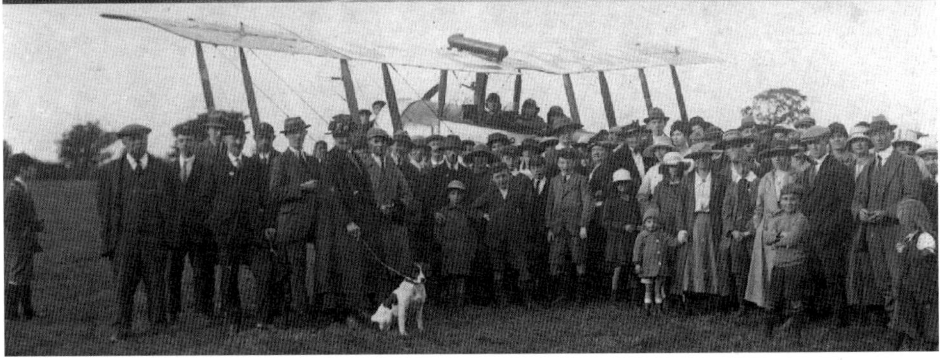

This picture shows the crowd that gathered in the fields between Whipton and Pinhoe to witness the novelty of the flying circus. Aviators like Alan Cobham would tour the country visiting different towns to offer members of the public the opportunity to try the new experience of flying. Below are the pupils of St Helena's School that was at 7 Church Hill. The principal was Miss Anita Brown-Paul and the lads who lined up included Michael Yendell, Ashley Walker, Richard Hutchings, Darch, David Houghton and Christopher Lamacraft.

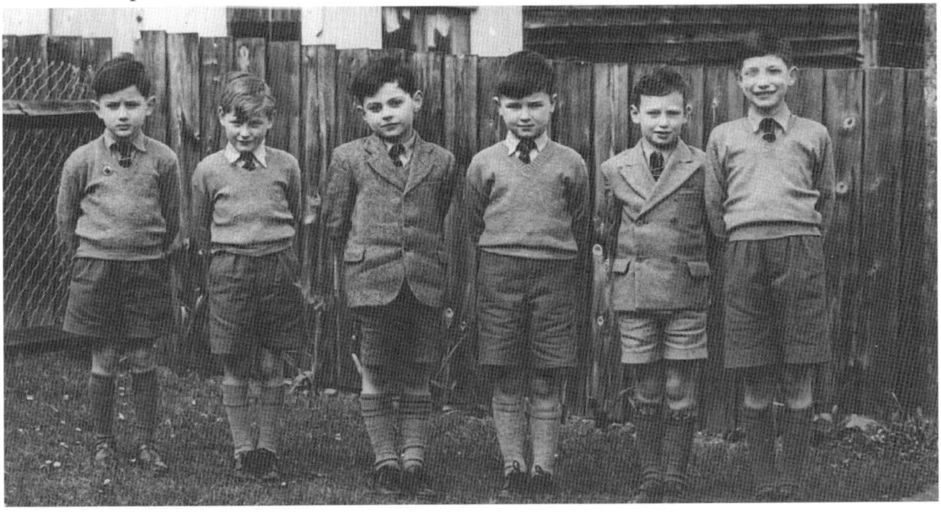

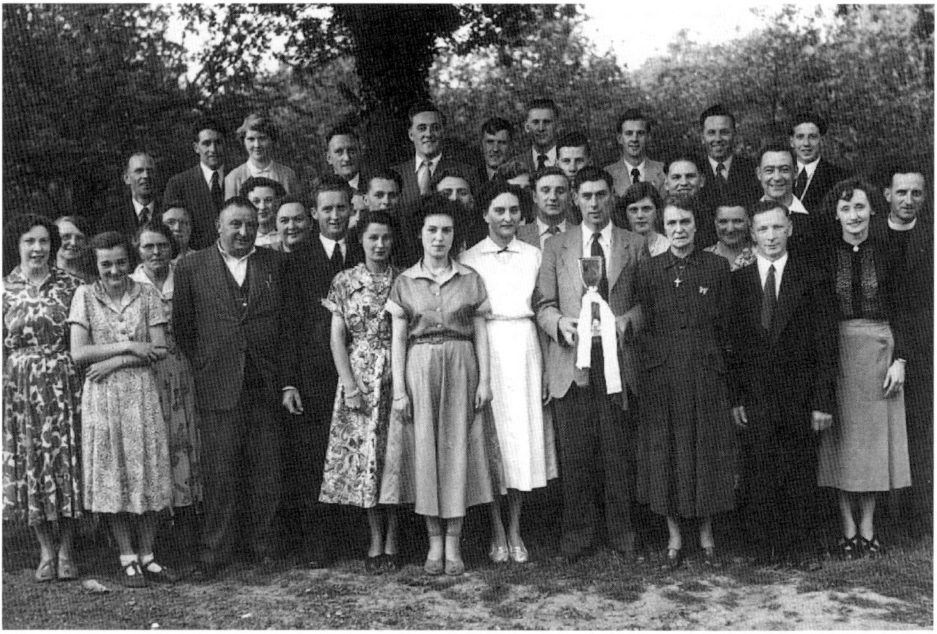

The top picture was taken in April 1952 and shows the late Percy Brook proudly holding a soccer trophy. The Rev F. A. J. Matthews is on the right hand edge of the photo. Below is a gathering of Pinhoe Youth Club in the Temporary Hut for their New Year's Eve party in 1948.

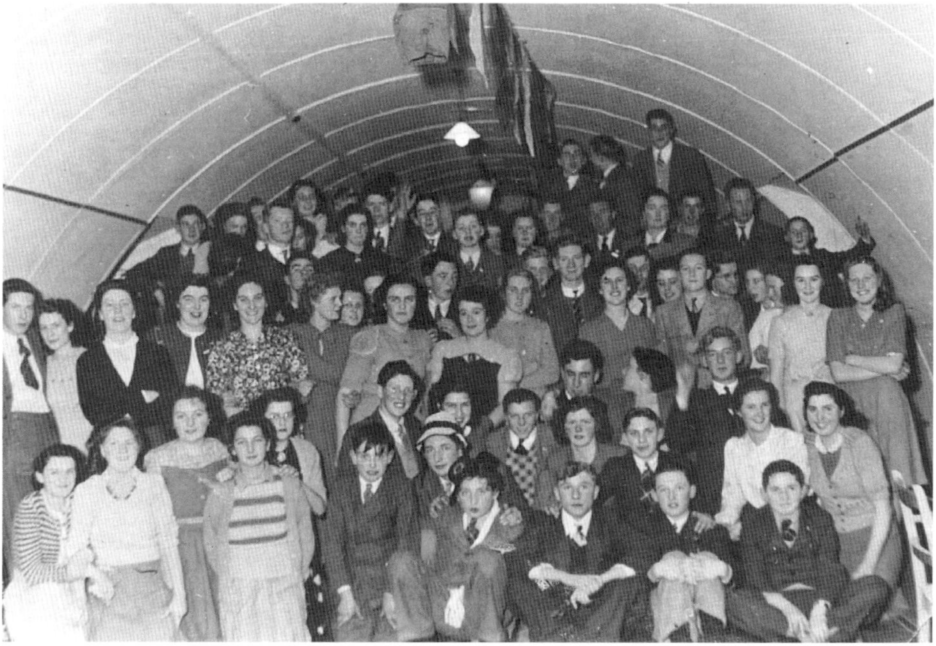

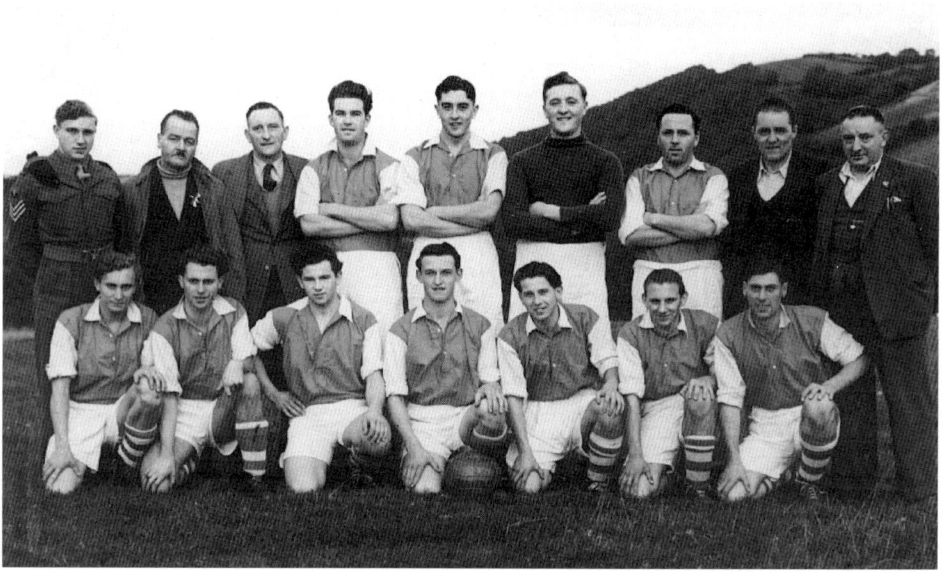

Here we have two soccer teams from Pinhoe's past, dating back to about 1949. The players in the team, pictured above, are – Back row (L to R): George Bauer jnr, Alfie Seager, Herman Bauer snr, Norman Gill, Jim Cowling, Boy Bauer, Frank Wellsman, Dick Rogers, George Bauer. Front row: Peter Brown, Colin Orton, Ivan Moore, Cyril Priddle, Ron Coles, John Taylor, Percy Brook. Nobody can recall where the top picture was taken but Chagford has been suggested.

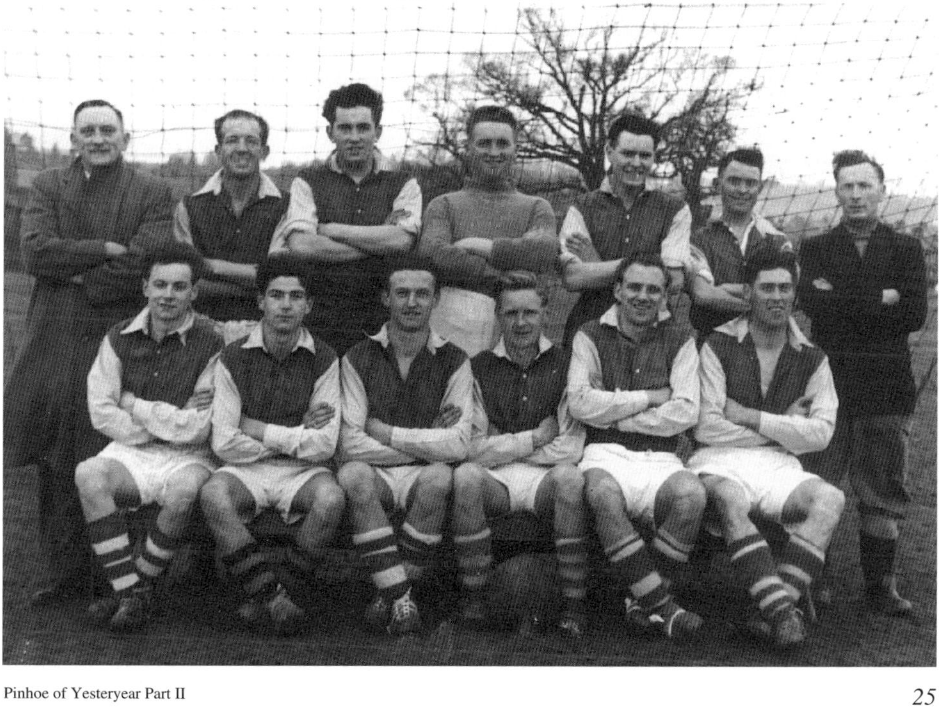

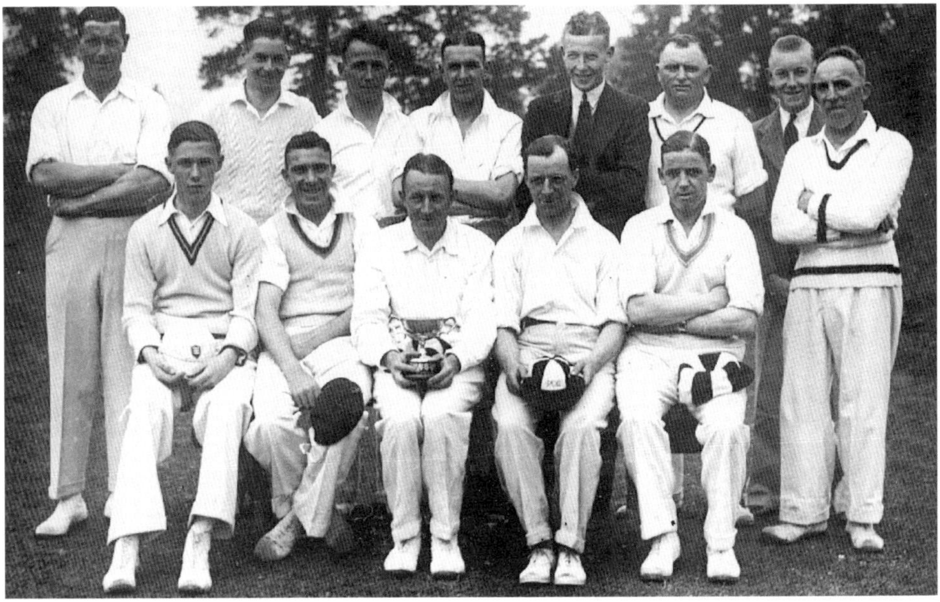

Pinhoe's Cricket Club have enjoyed success on a number of occasions. The above team were the Exeter & District League winners, Division 3 in 1936 and Runners-up Division 2 in 1937 when this was taken. Pinhoe's proud cricketers, from another team of yesteryear, are seen here posing for a team photo. As far as we have been able to find out the following players are lined up here – Back row (L to R): Robert Franklyn, Harold Cheeseman, Peter Allum, Percy Brook, Johnny Glanfield, David Burgoyne and Charlie Garroway. Front row: Bailey, David Trease, Plume, Des Fleming and Owen Easterbrook.

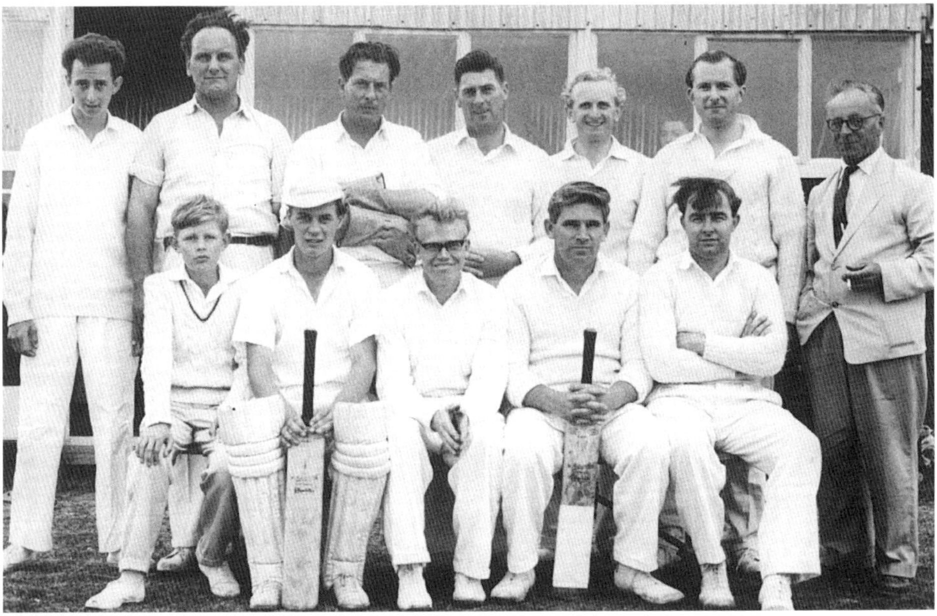

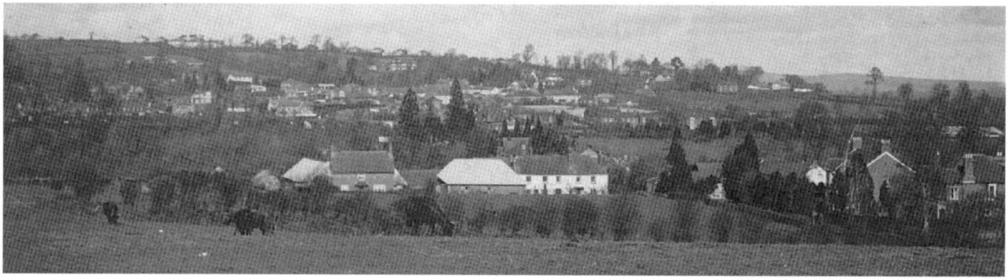

It's not much of a photo but is worth its inclusion because it will never be the same again. If you look closely it will be noticed that Pinhoe is punctuated with many open spaces that have since been developed. This shot was taken from the hill that looks down on Monkerton. The church was the venue for the crowd scene below. These children below were photographed in the grounds of a cottage almost opposite the chapel at Monkerton.

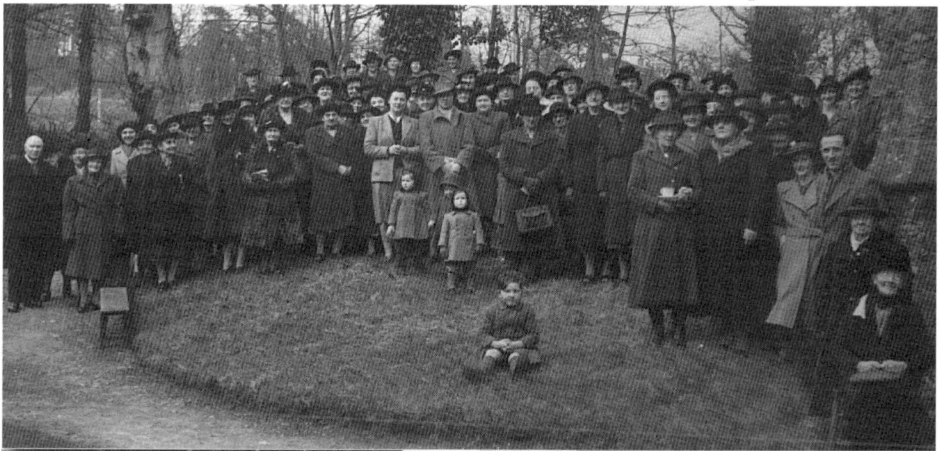

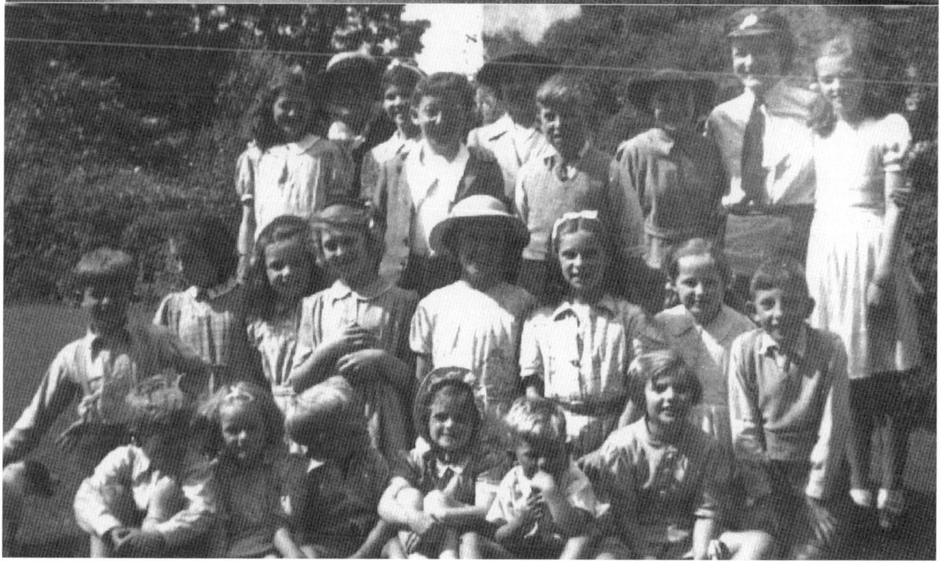

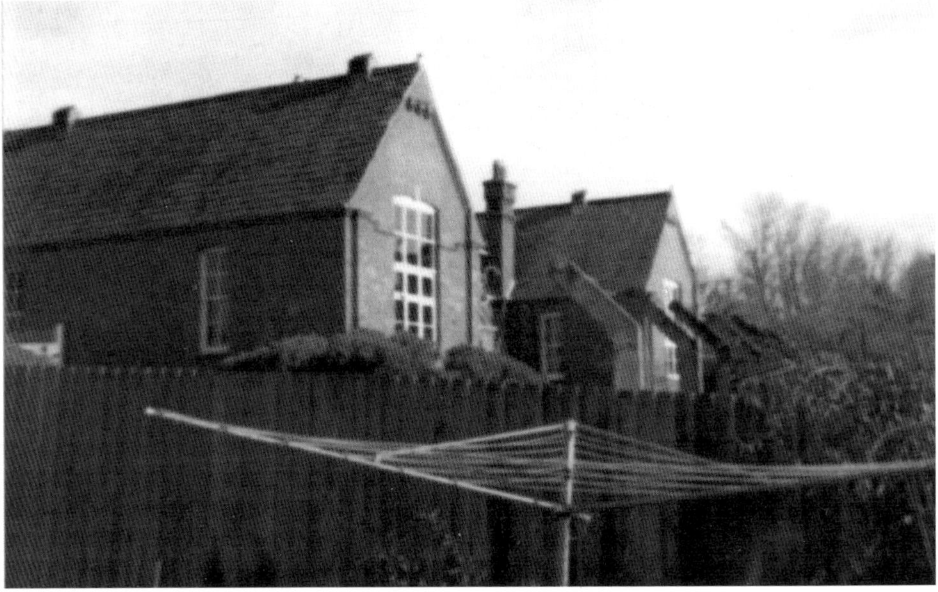

Pictures of the buildings of Pinhoe's previous school have proved to be few and far between. This slightly blurred picture is taken looking over the garden fence at the back of one of the properties along the main road. It should revive memories for those who spent their formative years there.

Below a garden party in the grounds of Broadfields saw an enthusiastic turn out of youngsters in fancy dress.

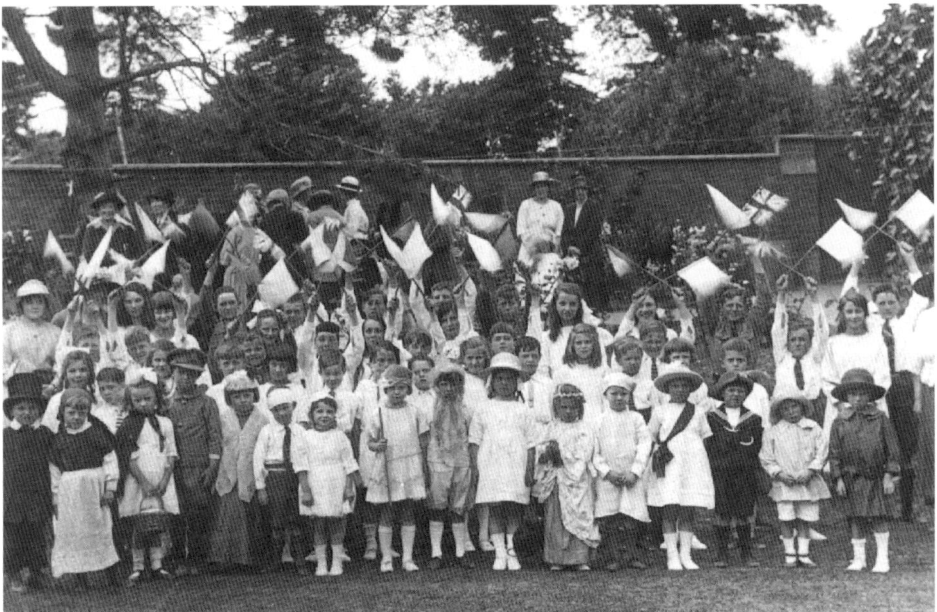

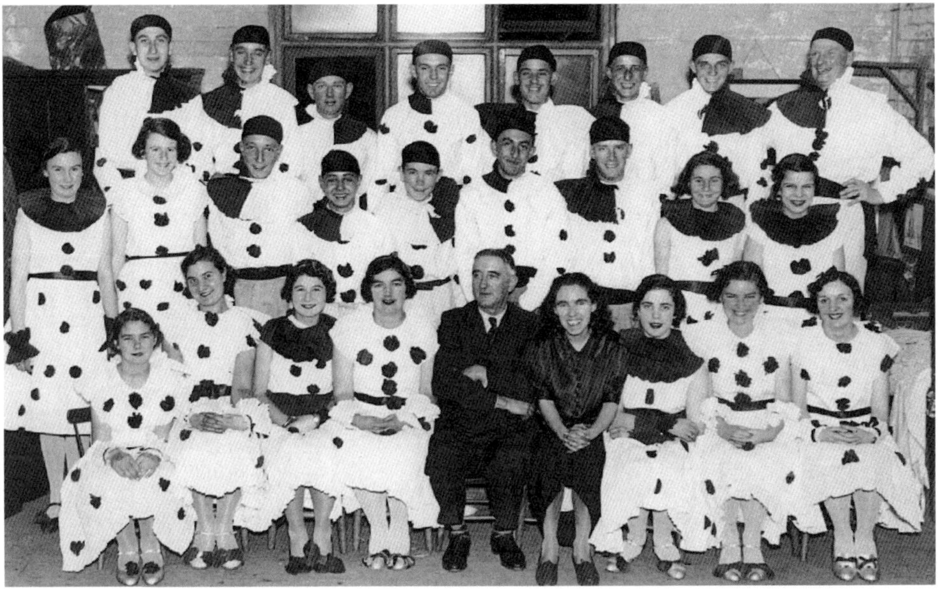

Are you seeing spots before your eyes? In the 1930s a Pierrot play was staged at Pinhoe School. The Headmaster was Mr Jones and his assistant Miss Parry is sat beside him. Below is Pinhoe AFC in 1925/26. Back row (L to R): Bill Joslin, Mr Browne, Bob Stile, Bert Westcott (Poltimore Arms). 3rd row: Mr Rowsell, Bill Harvey, Dick Bauer, Herman Bauer, Steve Lambert, Mr Rudd. 2nd row: Tom Bauer, Len Turner, Basil May, Frank Orton, Reg Stile. Front: Norman Parsons and Jim Vicary.

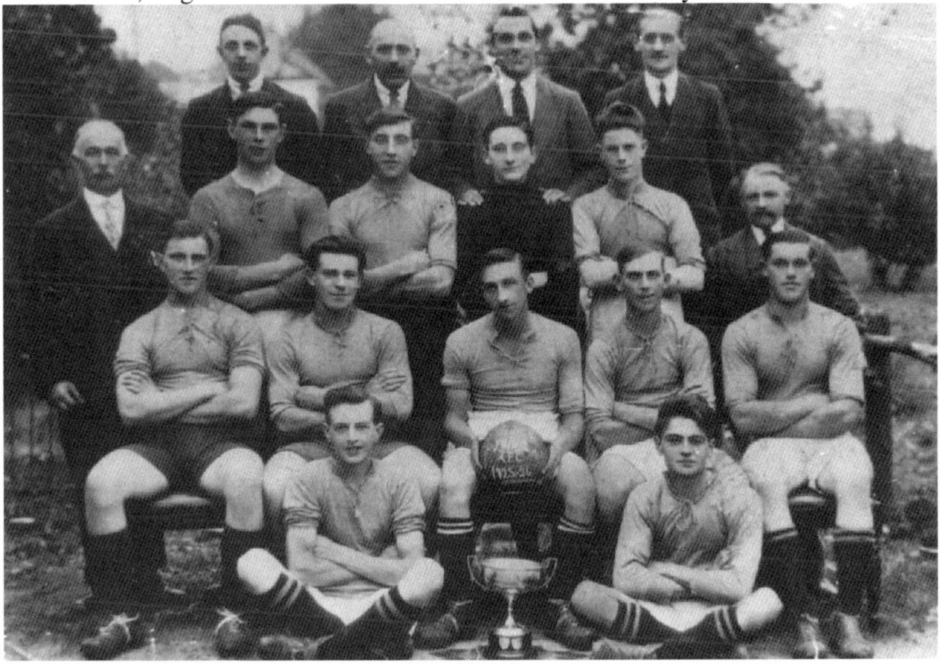

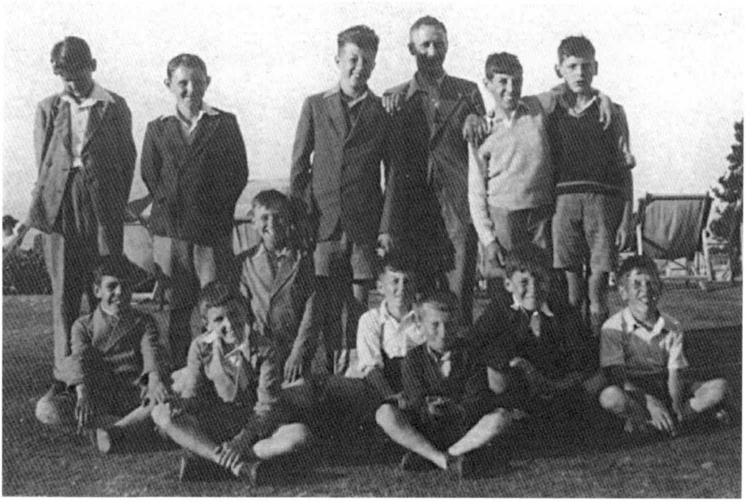

Here is an outing to Babbacombe for a group of Pinhoe lads. The back row shows Bill Taverner, Arthur Davis, Norman Davy, Mr Hopping, Frank Potter and Bill Pride. Front row: Gordon Browning, Holding, unknown, Arthur Butt, Raymond Hobbs, Bernard Rendell whose dad then ran the Poltimore Arms, and Peter Allum.

Ron Brealey lived at 9 Bradfield Road from 1954-1966 and, along with many other residents on the estate, was involved in organising bingo sessions and Saturday night dances at America Hall. The music for these dances, held in the late 1950s and early 1960s, was provided by a group called the "Semi Quavers". The profits went towards funding Fancy Dress competitions like this and setting up Christmas parties for the children of the estate. The monies raised meant that Father Christmas visited Pinhoe and bestowed each child with a gift. The photo included here was taken in 1960.

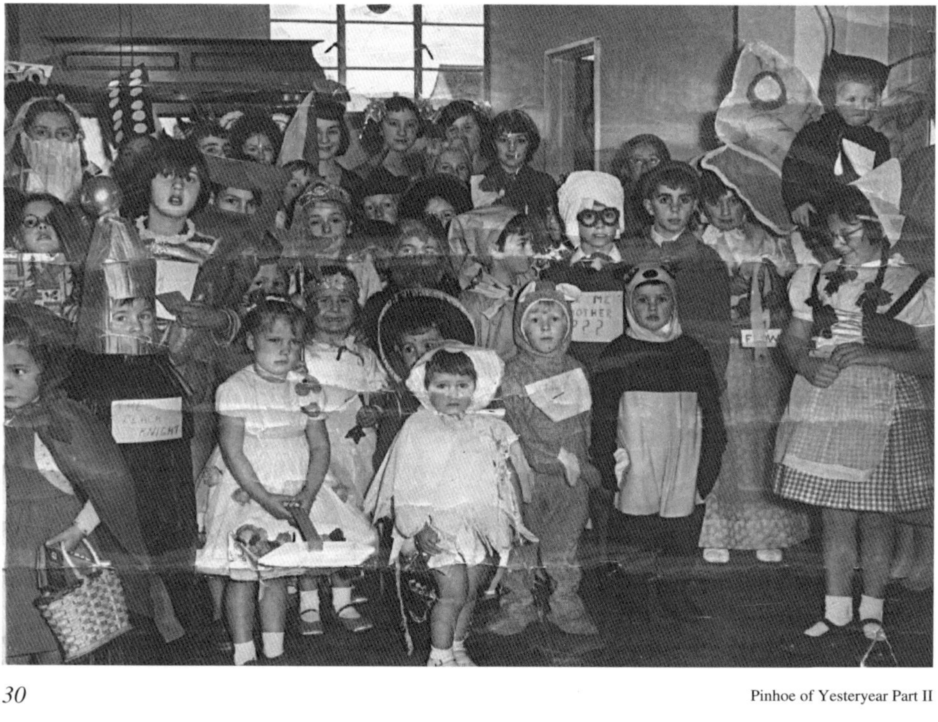

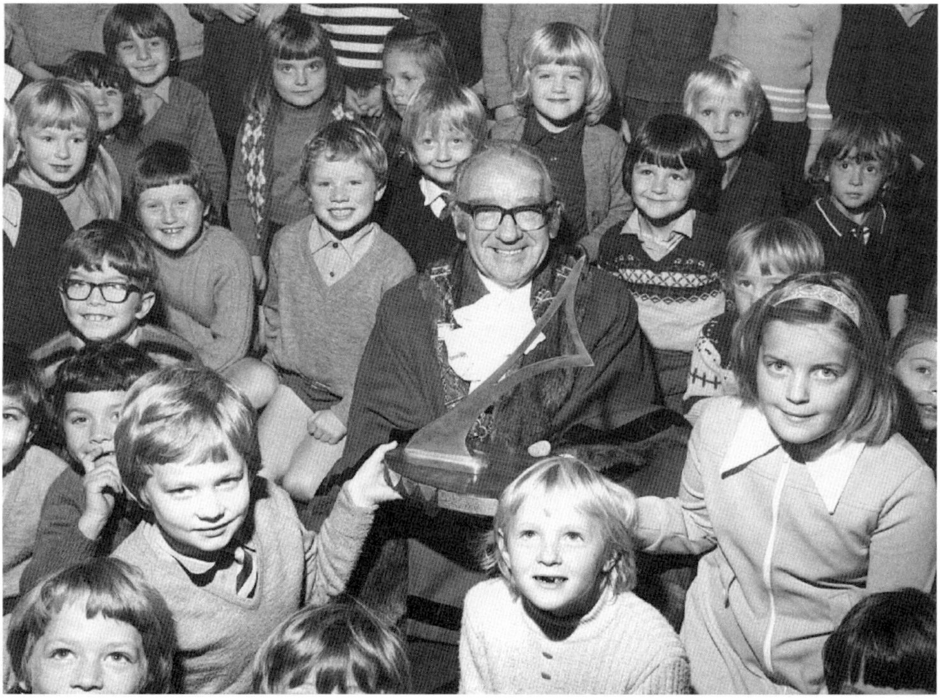

Above, the Mayor of Exeter, Mr Sam Honeywill, is shown with the children of Pinhoe School on 21 November 1974.

Pinhoe has had an enthusiastic Women's Institute for a good many years and pictured below are just some of their stalwart members being photographed at a time when they were in full anticipation of a good meal to follow.

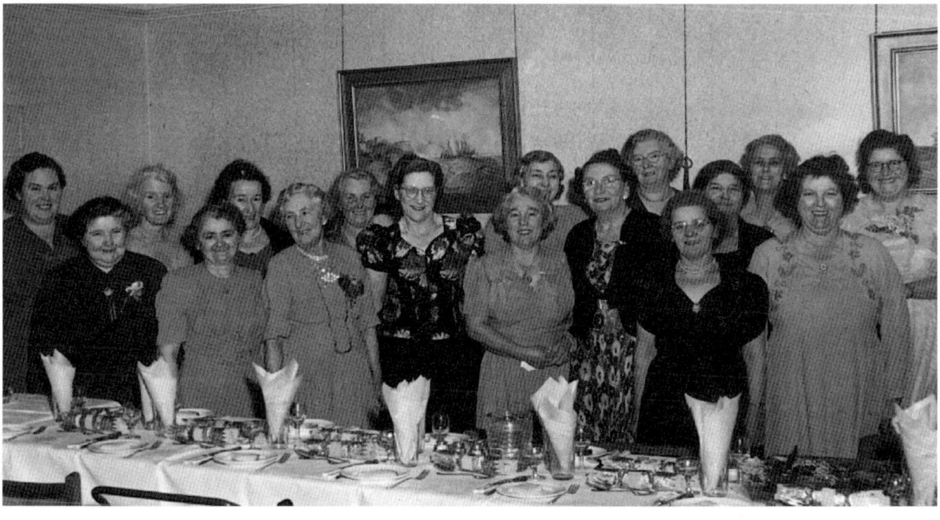

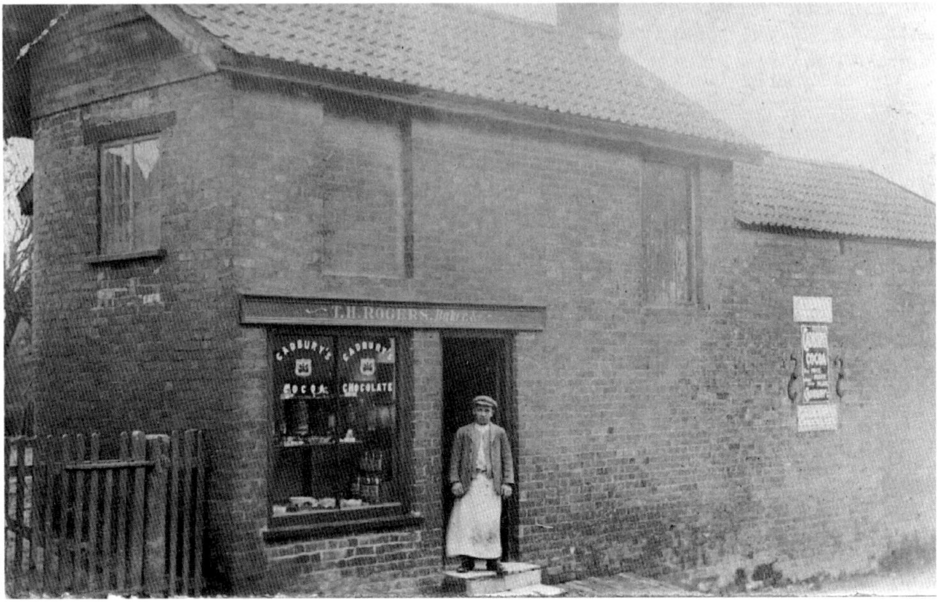

Joe Rogers, from the present ironmonger's shop, beside Spar, had the bedroom window in this picture. Stood outside is his uncle, Frank Rogers. The shop has long gone but was between the top of Station Road and the Hall Church.

The final picture looks from the Exeter side of the centre of Pinhoe towards the Poltimore Arms in an age when Pinhoe was much more of a country village. The pub is the only building that has survived since this picture was taken. Hope you enjoyed this selection that shows that nothing stays the same for very long!

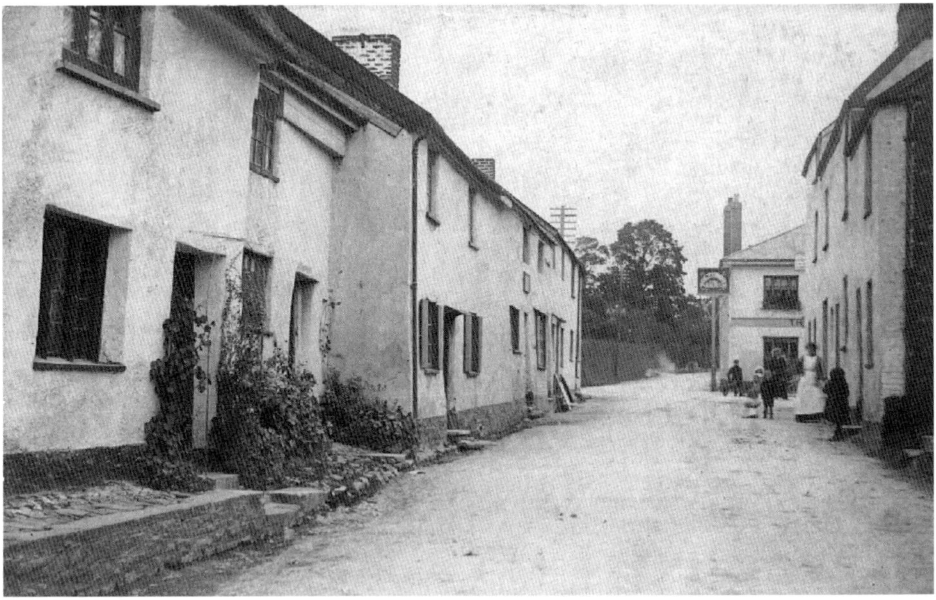